WHAT ARE THE LEADING CAUSES OF
LIFE?

**A Prescription
for Living at Your Highest and Best**

Therman E. Evans, MD, PhD

Copyright © July 2006 by Therman E. Evans, MD, PhD

Reprint, 2017   ISBN: 9780978950811

All rights reserved. Printed in the United States of America. No part of this publication may be reproduced or transmitted in any form or by any means without written permission of the author.

This Book is dedicated to:

God through whom all things are possible. My father, Irvin Evans, Sr. (deceased) and my mother, Constine Evans who raised and instilled in me a love for God, myself and family.

My wife, Bernetta Jones Evans for her love, wisdom and support over the past 40 years.

My two sons, Therman Jr. and Clayton Ennis
My daughter-in-law Monica Grant Evans
My granddaughter Taylor Naomi
and grandson Mitchell.

Special thanks to the following people for their invaluable assistance in making this book happen:

Julette Millien
Christopher Kelly
Peggy Ann Porter

ACKNOWLEDGEMENTS:

Carla Pope
Richard Holcomb
Veronica Holcomb
Carvetta Freeman

What are The Leading Causes of Life? is the first of what will be a series of "Prescriptions" to maximize one's life utilizing an approach that includes the "whole" human being, spirit, mind, and body.

To learn more about and/or request other publications by Dr. Evans please log onto his website - **www.drthermanevans.com** or write to:

Dr. Therman Evans
1009 Chandler Avenue
Linden, New Jersey 07036

Contents

Preface……………………………………..………i

Chapter 1
    Introduction………………………..…..……..1

Chapter 2
    Everything God Made
    Works…..................................……..……....12

Chapter 3
    Everything God Made **Has Everything It Needs**
    To Work……...........................……………...…51

Chapter 4
    Everything God Made **Was Made**
    To Do Work………………….........………..88

Chapter 5
    Everything God Made **Was Made To Work At Its**
    Highest And Best Through Relationship With
    Everything Else God
    Made…..………………….…..……………...126

Chapter 6
    Conclusion………………….…..…..……..166

Contents

Preface...i

Chapter 1
Introduction.......................................1

Chapter 2
Everything God Made
Works...12

Chapter 3
Everything God Made **Has Everything It Needs To Work**..51

Chapter 4
Everything God Made **Was Made To Do Work**...................................88

Chapter 5
Everything God Made **Was Made To Work At Its Highest And Best Through Relationship With Everything Else God Made**......................................126

Chapter 6
Conclusion.......................................166

Preface

Since writing this book several years ago, there have been many occasions for me to read and re-read its contents. And, whenever I have done so, I was reminded of how I felt when I originally wrote the book.

I clearly remember feeling like I had received a revelation from God.

Thinking about God and how awesome God is, four simple, but, to me, profound points became clear:

> *Everything God made works*
>
> *Everything God made has everything it needs to work*
>
> *Everything God made was made to do work*
>
> *Everything God made was made to work at its highest and best through relationship with everything else God made.*

These four points are simple but easily applicable as principles that govern the functioning of God's universe. And, as such, not only could be, but should be applied to our individual lives.

To the degree there is an understanding and application of these basic truths to one's life, success occurs.

These truths instill a calm, comfortable, and confident faith in who you are, why you are here,

what you are here to do and your ability to accomplish it.

They build self-value, self-worth and self-esteem.

They enhance optimism and enthusiasm.

They inspire energy and effort.

They grow courage and confidence.

Over the years since its original publication I have received many comments, feedback and reflections on and about this book. In each case it was always something that made a big difference to the reader.

Comments and reflections I've heard include things like:

... It was life impacting!
... It was life changing!
... This was extremely insightful!
... This was profound!
... More people need to see this!
... More people need to read this!
... Powerful!
... Awesome!
... Everybody needs to read this book!
... This was very helpful to me.

God is Life. The purpose of life is life and more abundant life.

Everybody wants Life. Everybody wants abundant life. So, it seems to me , to achieve the most life, our focus should be on the source of life and, how "The Source" works.

That is what this book is about.

Here are a few suggestions to get the most out of this book:

- ✓ Affirm out loud those phrases that resonate wherever and whenever possible

- ✓ Some phrases and sentences are repeated purposefully – read them with intention and focus

- ✓ Read with a group – this is always beneficial. Read with your family, ministry, church, friends, business or organization. The group can help encourage, inspire, support and/or make suggestions for specific activities to bring the message to life in your life

- ✓ Record questions and insights as you read, for later reflection and/or discussion

- ✓ As you read, think of ways you can put the principles in this book into action in your life…and then take action daily.

Please write and share with me your feelings about this book. I would like to know what has been responsible for you enjoying more life.

Chapter 1
Introduction

WHAT ARE THE LEADING CAUSES OF LIFE? This is a wonderful question. But, it virtually never gets asked. Rarely, if ever, do you hear this question asked by anyone anywhere. Yet, it seems to me, it is a question to which many would love to have the answer. At least, the question is worth asking and thinking about.

I have asked this question of literally hundreds, even thousands of people. The responses have been interesting. When asked, "What are the leading causes of life?" people often experience an immediate confusion. They don't quite understand what's being asked. Usually, further clarity is sought. I'm asked, *"Well, what do you mean or how am I supposed to respond to that or do you mean physical and tangible or spiritual and intangible?"*

The thing that is so fascinating about this confusion and the accompanying question is, there is never confusion or uncertainty when it comes to the opposite question, "What are the leading causes of death?" When asked to list the leading causes of death, people virtually always immediately start putting together a list. There is no hesitation, no confusion, and no question. Nobody ever asks me to explain what I mean by the question. Nobody asks me to explain what I mean by "death." Nobody asks what I mean by "causes."

A Prescription of Living at Your Highest and Best

People seem to be clearer about death and its causes than they are about life and its causes. People seem to be clear that if and when you do certain things, you increase your chances of death. People seem fairly clear that certain lifestyle behaviors will cause death. There is clarity about the behavior, and there is clarity about death. It's interesting to me that our society seems to be clearer about cessation (death) of life and its causes, than enhancement of life and its causes. Yet we are on a constant quest for as much life and living as possible. What a paradox. Abundant life and living is what we want and seek but we're not as clear about what causes it as we are about what causes death.

When asked the question, "What are the leading causes of life?" people rarely, if ever, put material wealth or things at the top. In fact, material wealth is usually not even near the top.

Most frequently mentioned at the top or near it is God. People seem to instinctively know and/or feel that there is an all powerful, all knowing, all loving Supreme Being responsible for the wonderful gift of life. Additionally, the top responses usually include things like love, family, peace, relationships, joy, work and a strong spiritual life.

Personally, I am convinced that God is life. The Spirit of God is life. The Spirit of God brings life. The Spirit of God causes people to come to life and, the life resulting from the presence of the Spirit of God is not a function of anything else outside of itself. It just is, period.

The leading cause of life is God.

The leading cause of life in humans is to know God. God is the source of life. God is the creator of life. God is the author, refiner, and finisher of life. God is life. It makes sense to me that, to learn about life and its causes, it is wise to go to the source. God is the source of life. God is the overarching intelligence responsible for the inception, maintenance and maximization of life of the universe, the life of earth, the life on earth including and especially the life of humans. **The leading cause of life in humans is to believe in and know God.**

Because you visit a hospital does not make you a doctor or a nurse. Because you visit a bank does not make you a banker but if you decide to connect with health care and/or banking by going to a school of nursing, medicine or business, the necessary education, training and relationships to be a health professional or banker can be accomplished. Then, after a sufficient amount of time you reach the point where you not only understand health care and/or banking, you actually are a nurse, doctor or banker. You achieve the new status of life as a health care professional and/or banker. Through a process of exposure, teaching, experience and time, the life of a nurse, doctor or banker can be accomplished. So it is with life.

If medical schools, business schools, hospitals and banks are the source of understanding and achievement in medical care and banking, then God is the source of understanding and achievement in life. This is accomplished through exposure to

God, teaching from God, experiencing God and time with God.

There are three ways to learn about something. They are:

1) the **words that explain** that something
2) **the work** that helps you understand the explanation of that something and,
3) **experiencing the doing** of that something.

We learn about God and we learn from God through His words, works and process. His word is scripture, His work is nature (including humans) and His process unfolds through experiencing Him. The best appreciation and grasp of life then, emerges through a careful study of scripture, nature and our personal experiences with God. To best understand and achieve life, give attention to its source, God. The best way to accomplish this is to give attention to God's words, God's works and your personal experience with God.

God's words all speak to life and how to achieve it in abundance. God's works all revolve around the production of life and our personal experiences with God are all life promoting, life enhancing and life enlarging.

It seems to me not a big leap to say, **the more and better you know God, the more and better you know yourself.** Humans are God's work. Humans are reflections of and representatives of the life producing work of God.

So, **knowing God is essential to knowing yourself.**

Knowing yourself (including being comfortable with and loving yourself) **therefore is a leading cause of life.**

I have always been a fairly active person. Some might even describe me as an "activist." At least I've participated in some of the major demonstrations of my time including the marches on Washington, beginning with the one now famous for Martin Luther King, Jr.'s "I Have A Dream" speech. I have never hesitated to speak out against racism or discrimination in public or private. But, a good portion of my 'activism' and 'speaking out' was grounded in anger. And a good portion of my anger resulted from my insecurities and feelings of inadequacy.

These feelings began to fade as my faith in God grew. This is as it should be, as I believe, insecurity and feelings of inadequacy cannot occupy the same space with faith in God. As my faith in God grew, not only did my sense of insecurity and inadequacy fade, but my sense of assurance, peace and knowledge of self, flourished. As my sense of assurance, peace and self-knowledge grew, I became more of an activist and began to enjoy life more and I began to enjoy more aspects of life.

This new life was manifested first of all by less worry, anxiety and distress with regard to societal and personal issues and challenges. Second, I found that, with less worry and anxiety, I had much more energy or life to put into challenges I was confronting. Third, with less distress, worry and anxiety, I could bring life to more things. So, in my view, knowing God and thereby yourself, is the leading cause of life.

I came to this conclusion based on observations of the life (nature, including humans) all around me. For many years I lived with my family in a wooded area just outside of Philadelphia. I had plenty of opportunity to observe the activity of many parts of nature. In seasonally appropriate timing, we experienced the life activity of trees, bees, squirrels, spiders, raccoons, butterflies, grass, flowers, deer, birds, bugs, worms and even a few small fish in the creek that ran through the back yard.

One day, while looking out the window, I noticed what seemed to me to be a family of deer. There were two large ones and two little ones. All four were enthusiastically engaged in eating the plants (Hostas) that beautifully surrounded our patio. I knocked on the window and tried to wave them away. But, despite my efforts they just continued to eat. In fact, in response to my knocking on the window, the biggest of the four seemed to look up and directly at me through the window. It turned its head from side to side with sudden quick movements while keeping its sights directly on me. And then, seemingly nonchalantly, it went back to eating the plants.

As I was looking into its eyes, all I saw was innocence and purity and sincerity. I saw integrity. I saw a creature of nature doing what it was made to do and being what it was made to be. In the seconds during which our eyes were fixed on the other, it seemed to be thinking, and I imagined would have said, were it able, "Are you talking to me? You moved into my neighborhood and destroyed some of the best parts of my community. You didn't check to see who else or what else may have been occupying the space. And further, neither I nor any of my family and friends protested. We didn't complain to you or about you. And now, you're trying to wave me away. Please! Be serious!! I saw these plants as a small token of appreciation to us from you for the opportunity to move into our neighborhood."

I stopped knocking on the window and watched as they continued to eat until they were satisfied and moved on. While observing the deer and the additional surroundings of trees, grass, rocks, the creek, birds, butterflies and squirrels, it occurred to me that what I was looking at was an abundance of life. Further, I thought human beings had nothing to do with causing or bringing this abundance of life into existence.

In that instant I felt and am convinced, I had a God moment. I say this because it is in this moment that God made me see the simple, but to me, very profound truths, that **everything God made works**, everything God made **has everything it needs to work**; everything God made **was made to do work**; and everything God made **was made to work at its highest and best in relationship with everything else God made**.

These principles, in my view, are pillars, which govern the functioning of the universe. They describe what gives, supports, maintains, grows, develops, matures and maximizes the life of the universe, and nature, including humans. They express the fullness of life, the wholeness of life, the purpose of life and the relatedness of life.

At a minimum, I am hopeful this book will serve to inspire and or motivate all who read it. In fact, inspiration and motivation are two of the main reasons for writing it.

At the moment of my revelation "everything God made works" I felt like God was speaking directly to me and saying, *"I made you, you work, you have everything you need to work, you must do your assigned work and, you must work in relationship with everything else I made to achieve your highest and best."*

This revelation was a life changing inspiration to me. It gave me a tremendous sense of clarity and empowerment. I felt that not only was I being given a message, but also I was being given a message to give to others. What is the message? Life! What makes it happen? What contributes to it? What enhances it? What deepens it? What raises it up? What restores it? What enables it? What empowers it? What maximizes it?

It occurred to me that responses to these questions would not only be applicable and helpful with life in general, but also, with many of the specific important subsets of life, like health, emotional and intellectual growth and development, spiritual strength and maturity, and social skills (including family, marriage, relationships and effective interpersonal interactions).

What are the Leading Causes of LIFE?

My purpose then, for writing this book is to help facilitate a "life" consciousness, a "life" clarity and a "life" orientation in people, in families, organizations and institutions.
At least, I hope to start discussions about the difference a life consciousness and orientation can make. My hope is that the individuals, especially young people, and those young in a new venture or endeavor who read this will come away with:

- Inspiration and motivation to live the fullest, most complete, most purposeful and shared life possible;
- Insights applicable to their life or to the life of their new venture or endeavor;
- Principles that change the way they view, approach and handle issues and challenges;
- Observations that enhance self-value, strengthen self-esteem, increase self-confidence, and generate action;
- A sense of purpose, empowerment and passion.
- God is about life;
- Life is consciousness and orientation.

Hopefully you will find that at least bits and pieces of this book will be inspirational, helpful and/or applicable to you and what may be going on in your life at this time. Optimistically, the main points and principles may even serve as your life governing philosophy.
The main points/principles of this book, simple though they are, in my view, represent the

overarching principles governing the life functioning of the universe, the earth and nature, including humans. These main principles once again are:

1. **Everything God made works** *(fullness)*;
2. Everything God made **has everything it needs to work** *(wholeness)*;
3. Everything God made **was made to do work** *(purposefulness)*; and
4. Everything God made **was made to work at its highest and best through relationship with everything else God made** *(relatedness)*.

What these principles say to me is, **when it comes to life, we are fully equipped, sufficiently supplied, packed with purpose and all connected.** This applies to marriage, family, business, organizations, institutions, dreams and aspirations. This also applies to specific issues, challenges and problems.

My contention is, people who view, approach and handle things with a life consciousness and orientation, are noticeable. They stand out. They stand up. They stand for something. They are pleasant to be around. They are easy to work with. They are challenging to work for. They make a positive impact.

They are distinguished from those without this orientation. How? They are distinguished in attitude, in energy and in activity. They believe things can be done. They bring great energy to getting them done. They are willing to take bold steps to make things happen and, they always expect to succeed.

It seems to me, this is what life is about. **Life is about a belief that things can be done, enthusiastic energy towards getting them done, a willingness to take bold steps to make it happen and a confident expectation of success.**

If I thoroughly believe that I am made by the same perfect God/creator that followed a perfect process to make a perfect nature that works perfectly, has everything it needs to work, does the work it was assigned to do and works through relationship, **then I must believe that I work, have everything I need to work, must do my assigned work, and I must work in relationship with others.**

This belief embodies the essential causes of life, and the life orientation I have been discussing.

Chapter 2
*Everything God Made **Works***

It is an interesting observation to me that all of nature seems to value itself. I never get the feeling or sense that any part of nature ever questions its value or wonders why it's here.

Every bird, bee, wasp, ant, panther, tiger, butterfly, horse, deer, squirrel, tree, mountain, river, ocean, fruit or flower I've ever seen all appear to be completely grounded, comfortable, and even confident in itself, its worth, its value. Nature seems to know that it works perfectly because it was perfectly made by a perfect Maker. There is no need to or room for questioning its existence or value. Indeed, nature operates from the perspective that existence is value and value is existence. In this context there is only embracing.

For life to be life it really must be embraced. The ups and downs, the peaks and pits, the peace and stress, the power and pain, the gain and loss all comprise the electrocardiogram of life. They all must be embraced as a part of life. The only time an electrocardiogram (EKG) is flat is when the heart stops beating. This of course means death is occurring, unless things change drastically, immediately. Life is not a smooth flat line. Death is.

For life to be fully appreciated, all of it must be embraced. Life must be embraced. Life is experience. The experience of life is possible because of existence. Existence is value. Value is contribution. Contribution is experience. Experience is confirmation of existence. Embrace the experience of life. **Embrace your existence. This is an awareness that supports human self-worth.** It supports self-esteem. The life-worth, value and esteem of people should be grounded in this fact. **Everything God made works.**

This means to me, that if I exist, I am of value. I am worth a lot. If I exist, I am esteemed by God. If I exist, I am valued by God. My life is important to the Creator of all life. I was made by the Creator of the universe. The intelligence and power responsible for bringing the universe into existence also brought me into existence. This is an awesome thought. This is an empowering thought. It is a thought that places my value at the highest possible level. This says my worth is established by the 'maker' of man, not man.

Every human being should view their value in the context of God. If I see God as the reason for my being here, I am seeing myself in the context of my highest possible value. When I look at myself through the eyes of the Creator, I see supreme value. I see worth. People that look at themselves through the eyes of God must have high self-esteem. Esteem means to value highly, or to have great regard for something. The esteem and/or value of something is placed in it and on it by its creator.

In the human condition, parents, through whom children enter this world, are primarily responsible for passing on to their children the esteem and value with which they are held by God. Esteem and value can only come from a source that perceives and appreciates it. The perception and appreciation for the true value of any invention or instrument can only come from its creator.

The one who brings something into existence is the one who knows best its value. Matthew 7:6 says, *"Do not give dogs what is sacred; do not throw your pearls to pigs. If you do, they may trample them under their feet, and then turn and tear you to pieces."* Certainly this verse speaks to being careful about whose hands, hearts and minds into which you place things you consider to be of value. Efforts to do this can be a tremendous waste of time and effort. I think this verse can also be a warning to not allow 'others' to determine what is or should be valuable to you.

Esteem and value are built into the creation by its creator. So, if the creation wants to know its true value, it must hear from and/or know its purpose from its creator. Esteem and value are tied to knowledge of purpose. Ignorance of one's true self and purpose contributes to lack of and low self-esteem. Lack of self-esteem or self-worth is at the foundation of self-destruction. Everybody, including yourself, disrespects, mistreats, maltreats, discards or destroys that which is perceived to be of value.

People who do not perceive the purpose of something, cannot fully appreciate its value. When the value of something is not fully appreciated, not only can it not be maximized, it will be misused, even abused. As has already been stated, one's self-esteem/self-worth should be grounded and firmly established in the truth that "everything God made works."

Challenging assignments are achieved by people *who believe they can*. People with positive self-esteem/self-worth are people who believe they can. Whenever God gave out tough assignments in the Bible, God always first dealt with the individual being assigned.

Oftentimes, as is too often the case today, the person being given the assignment was somewhere wallowing in self-pity, no and low self-worth. After Moses was given the assignment to lead his people out of slavery to the Promised Land, he complained about one thing after another. God had to work first on Moses to help him see his purpose, appreciate his value and thereby live up to his potential.

Exodus 4:1-17 (NIV-Life Application):
Moses answered, "What if they do not believe or listen to me and say, 'The Lord did not appear to you'?"
² Then the Lord said to him, "What is that in your hand? A staff," he replied.
³The Lord said, "Throw it on the ground." Moses threw it on the ground and it became a snake, and he ran from it. ⁴Then the Lord said to him, "Reach out your hand and take it by the tail." So Moses reached out and took hold of the snake and it turned back into a staff in his hand. ⁵"This," said the Lord, "is so that they may believe that the

Lord, the God of their fathers—the God of Abraham, the God of Isaac and The God of Jacob—has appeared to you."

[6] Then the Lord said, "Put your hand inside your cloak." So Moses put his hand into his cloak, and when he took it out, it was leprous, like snow. [7] "Now put it back into your cloak," he said. So Moses put his hand back into his cloak, and when he took it out, it was restored, like the rest of his flesh. [8] Then the Lord said, "If they do not believe you or pay attention to the first miraculous sign, they may believe the second. [9] But if they do not believe these two signs or listen to you, take some water from the Nile and pour it on the dry ground. The water you take from the river will become blood on the ground."

[10] Moses said to the Lord, "O Lord, I have never been eloquent, neither in the past or since you have spoken to your servant. I am slow of speech and tongue."

[11] The Lord said to him, "Who gave man his mouth? Who makes him deaf or mute? Who gives him sight or makes him blind? Is it not I, the Lord? [12] Now go; I will help you speak and will teach you what to say."

[13] But Moses said, "O Lord, please send someone else to do it."

[14] Then the Lord's anger burned against Moses and he said, "What about your brother, Aaron the Levite? I know he can speak well. He is already on his way to

What are the Leading Causes of LIFE?

> *meet you, and his heart will be glad when he sees you. ¹⁵You shall speak to him and put words in his mouth; I will help both of you speak and will teach you what to do. ¹⁶He will speak to the people for you, and it will be as if he were your mouth and as if you were God to him. ¹⁷But take this staff in your hand so you can perform miraculous signs with it."*

People with no and low self-worth, first of all, do not believe challenging achievements can be accomplished. Secondly, and even more importantly, they certainly don't believe **they** can accomplish them. Therefore, God's first step is to deal with the one to whom He is giving the assignment.

God convinces **them,** "they work". It is clear throughout scripture that the message from God to all of His people, is "everything made by Me works." The message is emphasized that if God made you, you have a purpose and you can accomplish whatever that purpose is. The same message given to Moses was also given to Gideon. It was a message of self-esteem/self-worth. It was a message of purpose, and power to achieve that purpose.

> Judges 6:11-16 (NIV-Life Application):
> *¹¹ The angel of the Lord came and sat down under the oak in Ophrah that beloved to Joash the Abiezrite, where his son Gideon was threshing wheat in a winepress to keep*

it from the Midianites. ¹²When the angel of the Lord appeared to Gideon, he said, "The Lord is with you, mighty warrior."
¹³"But sir," Gideon replied, "if the Lord is with us, why has all this happened to us? Where are all his wonders that our fathers told us about when they said, 'Did not the Lord bring us up out of Egypt?' But now the Lord has abandoned us and put us into the hand of Midian." ¹⁴The Lord turned to him and said, "Go in the strength you have and save Israel out of Midian's hand. Am I not sending you?"
¹⁵"But Lord," Gideon asked, "how can I save Israel? My clan is the weakest in Manasseh, and I am the least in my family."
¹⁶The Lord answered, "I will be with you, and you will strike down all the Midianites together."

Jeremiah had to search within himself and hear from God regarding his purpose and worth. He felt inadequate to the task he was being assigned. But, after tapping into the message God was giving him, he found the strength to make it happen.

Jeremiah 1:4-10 (NIV-Life Application):
⁴The word of the Lord came to me saying,
⁵"Before I formed you in the womb I knew you, before you were born I set you apart; I appointed you as a prophet to the nations."
⁶"Ah, Sovereign Lord," I said, "I do not know how to speak; I am only a child."

What are the Leading Causes of LIFE?

[7] But the Lord said to me, "Do not say, 'I am only a child.' You must go to everyone I send you to and say whatever I command you. [8] Do not be afraid of them, for I am with you and will rescue you," declares the Lord. [9] Then the Lord reached out his hand and touched my mouth and said to me, "Now, I have put my words in your mouth. [10] See, today I appoint you over nations and kingdoms to uproot and tear down, to destroy and overthrow, to build and to plant."

Luke 17:21 says, "*...the kingdom of God is within you.*" **God's Spirit resides within us.** The Spirit of God which is synonymous with the kingdom of God, more than anything else, I believe represents empowerment. It represents the ability to achieve the purpose, worth and value it brings. The Spirit of God gives no vision without the power to bring it into existence. Everything God made works. **When what God makes does what God made it to do, it always works.**

Everything not made by human hands works. Water works. Oxygen works. Trees work. Clouds work. The sun works. The moon works. The earth works. Soil works. The oceans work rivers work. Spiders, caterpillars and silkworms work. Apples, oranges and watermelon work. Algae and plankton work. Wheat, corn, rice, barley and oats work. Fruits work. Vegetables work. Minerals work. Insects work. Animals work.

The overarching guiding principle that appears to govern the fact these entities all work is **they all do what they were made to do**. They seem to only know what they were made to do and be. And therefore, all their energy is focused on and revolves around doing and being what they were made to do and be. **Herein lies the essence, magnificence, beauty and majesty of all of nature (God's work), it does what it was made to do.**

There is no pretense, no fabrication or prefabrication, no put on or put off, no make-up or masking, no posturing or positioning, no performing or acting. Everything is what it is supposed to be, and does what it is supposed to do. This purity is why all of nature (God's work—things not made by human hands) is so awe inspiringly beautiful. Anything that is and does only what it was made to be and do is always a thing of beauty. The reason we have zoos is the magnificent beauty of animals. The reason we have butterfly farms is the magnificence and beauty of butterflies. The reason we create gardens are the magnificence and beauty of flowers.

The purity and surety of nature (God's work) supports life, as we know it. The purity and surety of nature (God's work) is why there is life. Everything God made works. Nature is integrous. It is honest, accurate and sincere. Nature behaves the same way, everywhere, all the time. **Nature does the same thing in the same way, everywhere, all the time.** Nature is dependable. It is reliable. It is responsible. It is available.

A message here is integrity. **Integrity, wherever and whenever it occurs, is magnificent, magnetic and mending. Integrity engenders peace** and nothing engenders peace like the elements of nature. Integrity is alignment.

Nature is organized around the singular purpose of life. Nature is whole. Nature can only be whole, aligned, honest, accurate, sincere, indeed, integrous. This is so because nature is a product of God who is whole, aligned, honest, accurate, sincere and integrous. Everything that comes from God reflects God.

A newborn infant is integrous. The newborn is not long from the creator. Therefore, everything it does is exactly and only what it is supposed to do. The newborn is completely innocent, completely integrous, completely magnificent, and completely magnetic. People are drawn to newborns. People experience joy and peace in the presence of newborns.

It is fascinating, actually funny, to watch fully grown adults interacting with infants. An infant can drive a group of sophisticated adults into a joyous frenzy by doing the very simple things that infants do, like smiling, reaching their hands out, laying their heads on our shoulders, identifying their nose, beginning to crawl or taking their first step toward walking. These things infants do in total integrity.

A Prescription of Living at Your Highest and Best

When a group of highly educated and sophisticated adults can be turned into a group of babblers making up words that make no sense, they must be in the presence a powerful (magnificent, magnetic and mending) force. When my two sons were born, I, my wife, other family members and friends found ourselves gathered around our children enjoying them, touching and kissing their cheeks and saying things like "ooochie, coochie, woochi, woo." We would repeat these sounds and other single simple phrases as often as we could especially when it brought a smiling reaction from the baby.

The experience is now being revisited through my one-year-old grandbaby. Our house is filled with the love, joy and peace of life when she does her simple, little things, like smiling, walking, pointing to her nose on command, lying on our shoulders or falling asleep in our arms. At this point in their lives, I see infants as completely wealthy. Everything is done for them. Everything is brought to them. They have unlimited numbers of servants and unlimited service. They have 24-hour room service seven days per week. They want for nothing. They only have to open their mouths, speak up, cry out and instantly a servant appears and begins figuring out what the baby wants. Infants are integrous. What you see is what you get. This is why they are so magnificent, magnetic and ending.

Francis Bacon once said, "Be so true to yourself, you can't be false to others." Shakespeare said in Hamlet, "This above all: to thine own self be true, and it must follow, as the night the day, you cannot be false to any man." Alfred Lord Tennyson said in Sir Galahad, "My strength is as the strength of ten, because my heart is pure." Matthew 5:8 *"Blessed are the pure in heart for they shall see God."* Psalm 25:21 "May integrity and uprightness protect me, because my hope, Lord, is in you." Psalm 41:12 "Because of my integrity you uphold me and set me in your presence forever." **Integrity is power. Integrity is strength.** Integrity is fulfilling. Integrity is life at its highest and best. Integrity promotes life. **Integrity promotes and sustains life.** Integrity is reliable. Integrity is dependable. Integrity is responsible. Integrity is innocent. Be integrous and live life at its highest and best.

God does nothing halfway. God does not make junk. God does not make mistakes. God does not practice. Whatever is made by God is a masterpiece." Made by the master of the universe, each of us is a piece from the Master, and thus, a masterpiece. The "Book" version of the Bible translates Ephesians 2:10 this way: "For we are God's masterpiece. He has created us anew in Christ Jesus, so that we can do the good things he planned for us long ago."

Everything God made works. Since humans are made by God, we were made to work. Indeed, our physical makeup indicates we were made to work. God, a perfect intelligence following a perfect process made us perfectly.

The human being at the moment of conception – when sperm meets egg – is the size of a dot of the letter 'i' or the period at the end of this sentence. Two single cells – a sperm and an egg – come together to form one live being. Each cell brings with it a body of information and knowledge and wisdom that represents a set of instructions and directions that are combined to create a singular path of growth and development.

Following the preinstalled genetic information instructions and directions encoded on a molecule of double stranded DNA, these two cells--sperm and egg-- are mitotically transformed into 75-100 trillion cells that are magnificently organized. There are 206 bones, and 634 muscles comprising our muscular/skeletal system.

The nervous system is comprised of three sections-- a central, peripheral and automatic section. The central portion essentially is based in the head and includes the brain and the twelve cranial nerves that govern the basic functioning of our five senses: sight, sound, smell, taste and touch. The peripheral portion contains the spinal column and thousands (estimated by some to total l00,000) of miles of nerves, that go from the spinal column to various muscles, blood vessels and organs of the body. The automatic portion includes the brain stem, the hypothalamic portion of the brain and the master endocrine gland, the pituitary. It controls the automatic functions in the body like breathing, heart beating, digestion, and the reaction to stress.

The brain weighs about 3 pounds and is essentially 75-80% water. Experts estimate there are somewhere between 50 billion and 100 billion neurons (nerve cells) in our brain. These billions of neurons are information processing units that are connected to each other through synapses.

A simplified version of the way information processing works is as follows: information (ideas, thoughts, revelation, feelings, calculations) enters the brain from our Spirit and/or through our senses (eyes, ears, nose, tongue, skin) is converted to electricity, travels from one nerve cell to another by being converted from the electricity to a neurotransmitter (a chemical) at the synaptic junction between one nerve cell and another. The information travels across the synaptic gap as a chemical neurotransmitter, and then, on the other side of the synaptic junction, the chemical is converted back to electricity and travels through the next nerve cell body and axon to its dendrites (branches) where this process is again repeated at each synaptic gap.

So then, the brain receives a perception (sight, insight, thought, idea, sound, smell, touch, taste) converts it to electricity, then converts the electricity to a chemical and back to electricity again until the end result of the information perceived is achieved.

It's estimated we have approximately 60,000 thoughts per day. It's further estimated that the large majority of the thoughts or thought patterns we had yesterday are the same today. With each thought comes an accompanying biochemistry. The body bathes itself in the chemicals called for by the thoughts or thought patterns we are experiencing. For example, thoughts of intense competition and struggle can lead to a release of adrenalin and cortisol into the blood stream. Whereas thoughts of love, family and intimacy would generate a different complement of chemicals.

The cardiovascular system is made up of a pump (the heart) the size of a fist placed in the left central region of the chest connected to a series of pipes (blood vessels) that stretch out and over the entire body. It is estimated that the heart beats about 3.5 billion times over an average lifetime. That's three and one half billion gifts of life. The heart beats on an average at 60-70 times per minute, 4,000 times per hour, and 100,000 times per day, and it never misses a beat. If and when it does, you know it, and, if it misses 2 or 3 beats, your body will discontinue its normal functioning.

The heart has its own built in electrical system that drives its pumping action. I find this to be amazing. Just as amazing is that one person's blood vessels, if connected end to end, would stretch for about 75,000 miles. The circumference of the earth is only 25,000 miles. So, one person's blood vessels connected end to end would stretch around the circumference of the entire earth, not once or twice, but three times. One for the Father, one for the Son, and one for the Holy Spirit. **Everything God makes works.**

The respiratory system is just as magnificent as the other systems. Automatically, we breathe somewhere between 12-14 times per minute, 900 times per hour, and about 25,000 times per day. We don't have to consciously think about it or remember to do it. This means, each day we

What are the Leading Causes of LIFE?

receive from our creator an additional 25,000 gifts of life through our respiratory system.

Our lungs breathe in the atmospheric air through the nose and mouth. The air travels down through the trachea into the bronchial tubes, into the bronchi into tiny air sacs called alveoli. There are hundreds of millions of alveoli. It is in these alveoli, air sacs, where an exchange takes place. Oxygen is extracted, taken out of the air flowing through the lungs, and deposited into blood flowing through the lungs to be transported to and used over the entire body. We breathe in about six quarts of air every minute.

According to the book "You, The Owner's Manual" by Drs. Roizen and Oz, the six quarts of air that we take in per minute, is enough to fill ten million balloons over an average lifetime. The other part of the exchange that takes place is the elimination of carbon dioxide. Blood flowing through the lungs brings with it carbon dioxide it has picked up from tissues over the entire body. The carbon dioxide passes from the blood into the alveoli, the bronchi, the bronchial tubes, the trachea and finally, out the mouth and nose, into the atmosphere.

The gastrointestinal system is 35-40 feet of piping extending from the mouth to the anus and including the esophagus, small and large intestine. We take food in through our mouths and begin the digestive process by chewing and/or swallowing it. Amazingly, the digestive system breaks food down to useable levels, and extracts needed nutrients. It is then transferred across intestinal walls and blood vessels' walls where it is picked up by the blood stream and transported to all parts of the body where it will be transformed into energy necessary to sustain life. In brief summary then, the gastrointestinal system interacts with food in the following way: takes in, breaks down, extracts, transfers, transports, and eliminates. **Everything God made Works.**

Our kidneys serve as blood purifiers, blood pressure regulators, blood cell producers, and water waste removers. There is a system of sense organs connected to our central nervous system. These sense organs serve as our primary interface with the environment. The senses are sight, sound, smell, taste and touch. The senses gather information from and about the outside world so that the brain can decide what to do about it. The eyes are the complicated structures that allow light, along with what the light reveals, into the body to make contact with the brain, which then interprets what is being viewed and decides what to do about it. The ears are responsible for sound and balance.

What was God thinking when he determined that the structure by means of which we hear, would also determine our balance? **Why combine hearing and balance? I wonder if it has anything to do with the fact that "Faith comes by hearing the word of God..."** (Romans 10:17)? **Could it have anything to do with the fact that "hearing" the word of God brings the faith that corrects the**

imbalance created by a state of fear in our lives?

The ears receive sound waves and convert them into vibrations as they travel to and through the middle and inner ear. Ultimately the vibrations are translated/converted into a nerve signal, which the brain interprets. **Everything God made works.**

The nose can detect odors in parts per trillion. The odor that the nose detects must, again, be converted into the language of the nervous system in order for the brain to determine the body's action/reaction.

Our skin is the body's largest organ. The skin protects, participates in healing, receives and sends messages to the brain, senses temperature changes and is responsible for the sense of touch. The skin has embodied in it nerve endings that convert and translate to the brain, messages received.

One of the most fascinating systems in the human body is the immune system. This system operates with a remarkable "built-in" intelligence. It protects the body from foreign and infecting invaders. When foreign bacteria make their way into the body, the immune system picks them up on its radar screen, identifies whether or not and how foreign it is, and then it attacks. When it detects them again, the reaction is even more immediate. The immune system, based on its memory, will produce the exact type cell it needs to specifically target the foreign invader. **Everything God made, works.**

This brief nutshell summary of some of the workings of the human body testifies to the point, everything God made works. The detail, specificity, interrelatedness and productivity of the body parts, organs and systems are simply awe-inspiring. This brief summary of a few of the human body structures and functions gives a glimpse of all that must occur for life to happen. It also says, where there is life, an incredible amount of activity is occurring to support it. Life comes from God. God made humans. God is the source of life.

What were humans made to do and be? According to the Bible, we were made to be the caretakers, guardians, managers, growers, developers, replenishers and stewards of planet earth, beginning with ourselves. We were made to do this with accuracy openness, honesty and sincerity. We were made to have dominion, subdue, replenish, be fruitful and multiply. We were made to do this, with innocence (i.e. open, honest, sincere), and competence (accuracy).

The human being is a tripartite/trinity existence comprised of spirit, mind and body. Gen. 1:26 says humans are *"made in the image of and after the likeness of God."* John 4:24 says, *"God is spirit, and they that worship Him must worship Him in spirit and truth."* We are Spiritual beings having a physical experience. **We are perfectly made by a perfect creator to work perfectly.**

Any instrument, tool, or utensil works best and is maximized when used as originally intended, that is, as the manufacturer prescribes. **The life,**

health and well-being of the tool, instrument or vehicle is maximized (in contribution, enthusiasm, and longevity) by appropriate use as prescribed by the manufacturer.

Humans, according to God's word, are spiritual creatures. There is ample evidence pointing to our essential spiritual nature.

First, the things that matter in life and bring us the most joy are the intangible but very powerful spirit related things. Faith and hope are intangible. Inspiration and motivation are intangible. Humility is intangible. Enthusiasm is intangible. Peace, patience and persistence are intangible. Compassion and kindness are intangible. Resilience is intangible. Integrity and faith are intangible. Unconditional acceptance and love are intangible.

All of these things, integrity, peace, patience, persistence, hope, kindness, compassion, resilience, enthusiasm, humility, faith, unconditional acceptance and love are intangible, but, they have a very tangible impact on the way we live. In fact, they represent the core of the way we were made to work. According to Galatians 5:22-23, when we yield to the presence and power of God's spirit, the result is "love, joy, peace, patience, kindness, goodness, faithfulness, gentleness, and self-discipline." This is the way God made us to live. This is the way we maximize our human condition and potential.

We are spiritual beings having a physical experience. **Humanity is most human when**

it is most spiritual. Humanity is at its human best when it is its spiritual best. Our maker made us to work at our highest and best by being spiritual first. When we live by the Spirit, we live the way God intended for us to live. **When we live by the Spirit, we maximize our human potential.** And, when we live by the spirit, spirit directs and empowers us to care for, grow and develop our mind and body. Spiritual people obey God's word. Spiritual people know that God's word calls for the health, healing and wholeness of his whole creation. Humans are the crowns of creation.

Further, it should be pointed out that the intangible drives the tangible. **What you don't see determines what you do see.** The things in life that drive us, inspire us and energize us reside in the invisible realm of the spirit.

A study of 5 years to determine what makes people successful, by the University of Chicago in the early 1990's, looked at the top twenty performers in various fields: tennis, Olympic swimming, sculptors, neurologists, mathematicians and concert pianists. The interviews included the person, their families and their teachers. The study concluded, emphatically, the extraordinary success of those people was due to drive, determination and desire, not natural talent. These things (drive, determination, desire) are some of the invisible, intangible forces of the spirit realm.

What are the Leading Causes of LIFE?

The Spirit of God always and only leads in one direction—towards our highest and best. **The Spirit of God always leads us to God.**

The perfection of nature, God's work, is incomprehensibly incredible. **Nature works perfectly.** Nature is the product of a perfect maker, God. Humans did not make nature. Humans are a part **of** nature, made to do our part **in** nature, to help sustain the health and well-being of **all** of nature. Psalm 19 (BV) 1-6 describes God's work: *"The heavens tell of the glory of God. The skies display his marvelous craftsmanship. ²Day after day they continue to speak; night after night they make him known. ³They speak without a sound or a word; their voice is silent in the skies; ⁴yet their message has gone out to all the earth, and their words to the world. The sun lives in the heavens where God placed it. ⁵It bursts forth like a radiant bridegroom after his wedding. It rejoices like a great athlete eager to run the race. ⁶The sun rises at one end of the heavens and follows its course to the other end. Nothing can hide from its heat."*

Chapter 38-41 of the book of Job describes the work of God and how it all works, and how it was made to work. Verses 4-15 of chapter 38 expresses this magnificently (Message Bible):

> 4-11 *"Where were you when I created the earth?*
> *Tell me, since you know so much!*
> *Who decided on its size? Certainly you'll know that!*

> *Who came up with the blueprints and measurements?*
> *How was its foundation poured,*
>   *and who set the cornerstone,*
> *While the morning stars sang in chorus*
>   *and all the angels shouted praise?*
> *And who took charge of the ocean*
>   *when it gushed forth like a baby from the womb?*
> *That was me! I wrapped it in soft clouds,*
>   *and tucked it in safely at night.*
> *Then I made a playpen for it,*
>   *a strong playpen so it couldn't run loose,*
> *And said, 'Stay here, this is your place.*
>   *Your wild tantrums are confined to this place.'*
>
> *12-15 And have you ever ordered Morning, 'Get up!'*
>   *told Dawn, 'Get to work!'*
> *So you could seize Earth like a blanket*
>   *and shake out the wicked like cockroaches?*
> *As the sun brings everything to light,*
>   *brings out all the colors and shapes,*
> *The cover of darkness is snatched from the wicked—*
>   *they're caught in the very act!"*

Inspiring and reassuring is the fact that the same God, the same intelligence that shaped our solar system, shaped me. The same God that formed the Nile River, Amazon River, Tigris and Euphrates

Rivers, and the Mississippi River made me. The same force that formed Mt. Everest, Mt. Fuji, Mt. Kilamajaro, The Rocky Mountains, The Smokey Mountains and The Appalachian Mountains also formed me.

The same creator that created the flowers, the birds, the whales, the Great Lakes, the oceans and the waterfalls also created me. Once again, God does not make junk, God does not practice, and God does not make mistakes.

Everyday each of us should begin our day by affirming, *"I am the real deal. I am made by God."*

Why is nature so awe-inspiring? Because all of Nature Works. And, it works at its highest and best. And, it all works at its highest and best only at what it was made to work at. All of Nature is designed to work towards one purpose, Life! Each part of nature is committed to making its specific contribution, playing its specific role - to the enhancement of the life, health and well-being of God's Creation. **Life is the purpose of nature! Life is the essence of God! Life is the purpose of God!**

Death is the ultimate in dysfunction-- nothing works! In death there is darkness, emptiness, shapelessness, fruitlessness and no regeneration or restoration or multiplication. Death is the cessation of things working. It is the cessation of life. **Everything made by God works**.

Humans, like the root of nature are made by God. Humans are a part of the same nature, created by the same intelligence responsible for our universe. Humans were made perfectly. We were made to work. As long as we do and are what we were made to do and be, we work perfectly.

Nature is self-growing, self-developing, self-adjusting, self-adapting, self-sustaining, self-maintaining, self-healing, self-producing, and self-reproducing. Humans were made to be the same: self-growing, developing, adjusting, adapting, sustaining, maintaining, healing, producing, and reproducing.

A healthy set of affirmations include: **I work! I am fully loaded! I have all I need to be all I can be!**

Humans are spirit, mind, and body. We are an interconnected, interdependent, and interactive composite of all three. It is my contention that, the most important and powerful aspect of the human condition is the spiritual.

The spiritual component of the human condition is the life force placed in us by God. It is an invisible, intangible, untouchable, yet very present power.

- ✓ Spiritual people are powerful people.
- ✓ Spiritual people are integrous people.
- ✓ Spiritual people do and are what they were made to do and be by God.
- ✓ Spiritual people know "they work". They are clear they are made by God and are just as clear everything God made works.

- ✓ Spiritual people work *"...and they work not by power nor by might, but by God..."* (Zech 4:6).
- ✓ Spiritual people are unlimited because God is their source. God is their Supply, and they believe that *"God will supply all their needs according to his riches in glory"* (Phil. 4:19).
- ✓ Spiritual people are unstoppable. No mountain is too high, no valley is too low and no ocean is too wide to stop spiritual people on a mission.

Anything that does its highest and best, at what it was made to do and be, is a thing of magnificent beauty and magnetic attraction.

Whenever people face extreme difficulty, they tap into the strongest part of their being, spirit. **Our spiritual self, though intangible, nevertheless, represents the strongest part of us.** Humans were made beings comprised of spirit, mind, and body. All three components were made to work. All three components work. However, in our natural, tangible, physical existence, the tendency is to pay more and most attention to our tangible and physical components. And so, we tend to know more about and better understand our tangible, physical parts than we do our spiritual part. This is unfortunate, but true. And yet, **when faced with our biggest life challenges, it is our spiritual part to which we turn.**

For example, when the World Trade Center was destroyed in New York City, it represented the worst act of terror ever to take place on American soil. The world was shocked. America was beyond shocked. People were overwhelmed with pain, sorrow, sadness, anguish, agony, distress, fear, and uncertainty. These were the feelings dealt with in the immediate aftermath of the terrorist tragedy.

The headlines of major newspapers, magazines and billboards across the country did not focus on whether or not America had the might, money, or manpower to rebound. These were a given. Nobody doubted that these things were present and available. The issue raised and focused on by the major national news was, "did America have the spirit to rebound?" Story after story, and headline after headline addressed the spirit of America. Political, educational, social, and economical organizations joined religious organizations in their efforts to tap into and strengthen the spirit of the people. Everybody was crystal clear that to survive and thrive following such a devastating event, peoples' spiritual strength would have to be fortified.

We are spiritual beings having a physical experience. **The true essence of the human experience is spiritual. Human beings are most similar, and make the strongest connections in the realm of the spirit.** Faith, hope, inspiration, motivation, humility, enthusiasm, patience, persistence, compassion, kindness, resilience, integrity, love, and unconditional acceptance all look the same, are expressed the same way and have the same impact no matter the person's race, ethnicity, culture, age or gender.

What this says to me is, **humans work best when they are most spiritual.** Humans are most effective and efficient when we are doing and being what we are made to do and be.

Nature works the same way and speaks the same language in all locations on earth. The sun over North America is the same sun that rises over Europe, Africa, and South America. Wheat in Australia and how you grow it is the same in America. A fish in Africa would be a fish in Japan. A tree in Europe would still be a tree in Asia. No matter what continent or country you are in, nature works the same and speaks the same language. Oxygen is the same everywhere on earth. Water is the same everywhere on earth.

The same is true for humans in a realm of the spirit. **No matter where you are on earth, things like resilience, faith, persistence, patience, unconditional acceptance, love and kindness all look the same, and work the same way.**

Everything God made, works.

The basis of the beauty of everything God made is, it is and does what it was made to do and be. This principle is responsible for the awesome beauty and inspiration of mountains, rivers, sunrises, sunsets, lakes, birds, butterflies, valleys, cloud formations, rain, rainbows, snowflakes, snowfalls, and fall foliage. And so, **a spiritual human being is beauty in action.**

The foundation of the principle of things "being and doing" what they were made to be and do is, order. I Corinthians 14:40 says, *"Let all things be done decently and in order."* In the 33rd verse of the same chapter it says, *"For God is not a God of confusion and disorder, but of peace."*

The first rule of the universe is, order. Without order you have chaos. Webster's New World Dictionary describes chaos as: the disorder of formless matter and infinite space, supposed to have existed before the ordered universe. The second definition is; any great confusion or disorder. Genesis 1:2 says, *"Now the earth was formless and empty; and darkness was upon the face of the deep..."*

In the account of creation in the first chapter of Genesis, the first thing God did was establish order. God took in his hands the formless, shapeless, disorderly, chaotic matter and space and gave it form, shape, structure, and indeed order.

Everything that God made, works. **Anything that works must have order.** Why? Because disorder is dysfunctional and does not work. Formlessness, shapelessness, emptiness, and darkness do not and cannot work. These things must be rearranged by purpose in order for them to "work". **Everything God made works because everything God made has purpose. Purpose is an organizing force.**

What are the Leading Causes of LIFE?

- ❖ **Purpose generates order and organization.**
- ❖ **Purpose brings form to formlessness, shape to shapelessness, and light to darkness.**
- ❖ **Purpose makes a positive contribution to life. Purpose moves things.**
- ❖ **Purpose establishes direction.**
- ❖ **Purpose provides meaning.**
- ❖ **Purpose empowers.**
- ❖ **Purpose informs and instructs.**
- ❖ **Purpose inspires and motivates.**
- ❖ **Purpose drives.**

When you determine purpose you have determined the reason for which something exists. **Anything that is and does what it was made to be and do is achieving purpose.** In other words, it works!

Everything God made works. Everything not made by human hands works and works perfectly.

The purpose of oxygen is to be oxygen and do what oxygen is supposed to do. The purpose of water is to be water and do what water does. The purpose of the sun is to be the sun and do what the sun does. The purpose of wheat, corn, and cabbage is to be wheat, corn, and cabbage and to do what wheat, corn, and cabbage do. The purpose of honeybees, birds, and butterflies is to be honeybees, birds, and butterflies and to do what honeybees, birds, and butterflies do. The purpose of whales, sharks, fish, tigers, ants, and panthers is to be whales, sharks, fish, tigers, ants, and panthers and do what they do. In every instance mentioned, purpose is achieved. It works. They work. It was made to work. They were made to work. It was made to work by God. They were made by God, and everything God made works.

Fish achieve their purpose in water. Vegetation achieves its purpose in soil. Flying birds achieve their purpose in the open air. In each instance, the entity has a structure, an order, an organization that is not only consistent with, but necessary to achieve their full purpose.

Likewise, human beings best achieve their full purpose through the realm of spirit. The formlessness, shapelessness, emptiness, and the darkness that too often characterizes human beings, results when we ignore our spiritual selves. **Human beings are always changed by spiritual purpose, God's original intention for us.**

When people walk in the spirit, live by the spirit and lead with the spirit they are both magnificent, and magnetic and mending.

All of nature works, and, it works perfectly. Life as we know it depends on it. The reason this is true is, all of nature simply does exactly what it was made to do. The success of nature lies in the fact that every aspect of it follows the prescribed plan preinstalled in it. In nature, there is no free will and/or independent thinking. **The operational instructions built into every aspect of nature are followed precisely.**

There is one exception to this rule, human beings. Humans are the only part of nature-as far as we know- gifted with powers of free will, independent thinking and spiritual strength. A panther only does panther like things. It never varies. Trees are only trees. They are never anything else. They never try to be anything else. **Human beings are the only part of nature that can actually be aware of what's best and should be done, and make a decision that's totally opposite.**

Imagine having a plan of success and making a conscious decision not to follow it. People do this often. We know what's best, we know what the right thing to do is, yet, we decide to do something that is opposite to it. This is the source of human disease, distress, discontent, disturbance and destruction. **Real life for humans is in the spirit. When people decide to walk in the spirit, live by the spirit and lead with the spirit, they are magnificent, magnetic and mending.**

> Matthew 6:24-33 (The Book) says:
> *"You cannot serve two masters. For you will hate one and love the other, or be devoted to one and despise the other. You cannot serve both God and money.*
> *^{25}So I tell you, don't worry about everyday life – whether you have enough food, drink, and clothes. Doesn't life consist of more than food and clothing? ^{26}Look at the birds.*

A Prescription of Living at Your Highest and Best

> *They don't plant or harvest or put food in barns because your heavenly Father feeds them. You are more valuable to him than they are. ²⁷Can all your worries add a single moment to your life? Of course not.*
> *²⁸Why worry about your clothing? Look at the lilies how they grow. They don't work or make their clothing, ²⁹yet Solomon in all his glory was not dressed as beautifully as they are. ³⁰If God cares so wonderfully for flowers that are here today and gone tomorrow, won't he more surely care for you? You have so little faith.*
> *³¹So don't worry about having enough food, drink or clothes. ³²Why be like the pagans who are so deeply concerned about these things? Your heavenly Father already knows all your needs, ³³and will give you all you need from day to day if you live for him and make the kingdom of God your primary concern."*

When people are and do what we were made to be and do, we succeed, prosper, enjoy and contribute to the enhancement of life. **We were made to be spiritual**.

A spiritual human being **is one who puts a first priority on the kingdom of God.**

A spiritual human being **is one who exercises dominion over his life, is fruitful, multiplies, has self-discipline and gives back or helps others.**

A spiritual human being is one who takes authority, and is alive, alert, and actively engaged in establishing and expanding abundant life.

A spiritual human being is liberated and unlimited.

> Daniel 3:19 - 25 (The Book):
> *[19]Nebuchadnezzar was so furious with Shadrach, Meshach and Abednego that his face became distorted with rage. He commanded that the furnace be heated seven times hotter than usual. [20]Then he ordered some of the strongest men of his army to bind Shadrach, Meshack and Abednego and throw them into the blazing furnace. [21]So they tied them up and threw them into the furnace, fully clothed. [22]And because the king, in his anger, had demanded such a hot fire in the furnace, the flames leaped out and killed the solders as they threw the three men in. [23]So Shadrach, Meshach, and Abednego, securely tied, fell down into the roaring flames. [24]But suddenly, as he was watching, Nebuchadnezzar jumped up in amazement and exclaimed to his advisers, "Didn't we tie up three men and throw them into the furnace?" "Yes" they said, "we did indeed, Your Majesty." [25]"Look," Nebuchadnezzar shouted! "I see four men, unbound, walking around in the fire. They aren't even hurt by*

the flames! And the fourth looks like a divine being!"

No matter how difficult or intense the challenge, spiritually strong and led people never give up or back down. People who know God and know themselves, are never afraid to pursue life. Life is unlimited, because God is unlimited. Therefore, it's important to let God establish your life boundaries. Do not let other people or challenging circumstances created by yourself or other people set your boundaries. Let God establish your boundaries. When God establishes your boundaries, you live a maximized life; you live an unlimited life. When God establishes your boundaries, you will come face to face with serious, even life threatening danger, but, the fact that you are within boundaries established by God, He will keep you assured, advancing and at peace. **Everything God made works.**

Humans were made by God to be spiritual beings. As such, we live unlimited and maximized lives. The point of this passage of scripture is the pursuit of life, never give up or back down from serious adversity. Imagine for a moment, a people or a person with the motto, "Don't give up and don't back down." Progress and fruitfulness are embodied in this motto. It is a major theme of scripture, which means it's a major theme of God, which means, it's a major theme of spiritual people.

Spiritual people declare, "even though I walk through the valley of the shadow of death, I will fear no evil because God is with me. His rod and His staff comfort me." When you let God establish your boundaries, God is your shepherd. Therefore, you shall not lack and you shall not be limited.

> Mark 11:1-7(The Book):
> *¹As Jesus and his disciples approached Jerusalem, they came to the towns of Bethphage and Bethany, on the Mount of Olives. ²Jesus sent two of them on ahead. "Go into that village over there," he told them, "and as soon as you enter it, you will see a colt tied there that has never been ridden. Untie it and bring it here. ³If anyone asks what you are doing, just say, "The Lord needs it and will return it soon." ⁴The two disciples left and found the colt standing in the street, tied outside a house. ⁵As they were untying it, some bystanders demanded, "What are you doing untying that colt?" ⁶They said what Jesus had told them to say, and they were permitted to take it. ⁷Then they brought the colt to Jesus and threw their garments over it, and he sat on it.*

A spiritual human being is "loosed and let go."

> John 11:38-44 (The Book):
>
> *³⁸And again Jesus was deeply troubled. Then they came to the grave. It was a cave with a stone rolled across its entrance.*

A Prescription of Living at Your Highest and Best

> *^{39}"Roll the stone aside," Jesus told them. But Martha, the dead man's sister, said, "Lord, by now the smell will be terrible because he has been dead for four days." ^{40}Jesus responded, "Didn't I tell you that you will see God's glory if you believe?" ^{41}So they rolled the stone aside. Then Jesus looked up to heaven and said, "Father, thank you for hearing me. ^{42}You always hear me, but I said it out loud for the sake of all these people standing here, so they will believe you sent me." ^{43}Then Jesus shouted, "Lazarus, come out!" ^{44}And Lazarus came out, bound in grave clothes, his face wrapped in a head cloth. Jesus told them, "**Unwrap** him and let him go!"* (Author emphasis)

There are very important messages we can receive from this account of raising Lazarus from the dead. The first is that spiritual people hear and respond to the voice of God. No matter how difficult the situation, spiritually strong people can hear the very powerful calling of God. No matter how far gone the situation appears, it is never too far gone for God, and God will call out to you.

The second message is God always speaks life. God always calls us to life. God always calls life to come out of the grips of death. If you stop and really think about it, each time you made it through what you felt was your worst nightmare, there was a spark of light, inspiration or motivation that occurred during the ordeal that made you know you would eventually make it through. Many times, if not most of the time, that spark – at least for me – was an intense fervent and frequent prayer to God for help. I dug down deep into my spiritual core, reached "in" to God and God responded by strengthening me to make it through.

The third message I received from this passage is you must come out of your grave on your own. Nobody can come out of your grave for you. **Everything God made works.** So, when God calls, requests, inspires or motivates us to do something, God knows it can be done, and the one being spoken to can do it. What the circumstances are do not matter to the spiritually led and spiritually empowered person. When God calls, speaks, requests, inspires or motivates, the spirit led and empowered person will respond.

Jesus taught His disciples to pray *"Our Father who is in heaven, Holy is thy name. Thy kingdom, thy will be done on earth as it is in heaven."* God does not teach people to ask for something that cannot be done or that cannot happen. Nor does God ask us to do something that we cannot do or that we cannot make happen. **If in your spirit, you think it should be done, or it can be done, or you hope it is done, you are probably the one to do it or be the instrument used to make it happen.**

When humans work like they were made to work, placing priority on and always leading with the spiritual, they are always at their highest and best. This means they are liberated and unlimited.

They are loosed and let go. **Everything God made, works.**

Chapter 3
*Everything God Made **Has** Everything It Needs To Work*

The 1st law of thermodynamics says: "energy in the universe is neither created nor destroyed but is constantly in the process of being converted from one form to another." This means the universe is a self-contained, self-sustained, self-adjusting, self-managing, self-healing, self-growing, self-developing whole entity. There is nothing missing. Everything needed for the universe to work at its highest and best was preinstalled and set in motion to last as long as it needs to.

What God makes is complete. God is a God of wholeness. To say that something is missing or incomplete in the universe is to say that God is incomplete, or has something missing. God is wholeness, completeness, perfection, and cannot act out of character. To know this is to generate love for God, peace from God, self-worth, self-esteem and self-confidence. Indeed, it should generate life.

Nature is self-contained, self-sustaining, self-adjusting, self-maintaining/managing, self-healing, self-growing, and self-developing. **There is nothing missing in nature.** Nature is whole. Therefore, nature can and does heal itself. Nature has all it needs to heal itself. As part of nature, made by the same creator, I believe humans are self-contained self-sustaining, self-adjusting,

A Prescription of Living at Your Highest and Best

self-maintaining, self-healing, self-growing, self-developing and can heal themselves. Jesus said in Luke 17:21, *"...the kingdom of God is within."* On other occasions Jesus reminded people that everything God made has everything it needs to work.

The woman with a twelve yearlong battle with an illness that had consumed her energy, time, patience, and all her money, came to Jesus convinced she would finally be healed. She came to Jesus convinced she would finally achieve what she had been unsuccessfully trying to achieve over the past twelve years. She reached and touched the hem of Jesus' garment and was healed. And Jesus said to her in Mark 5:34 *"Daughter, **your** faith has healed you. Go in peace and be freed from your suffering."*

When a blind man called Bartimaeus came to Jesus seeking his sight, he (Bartimaeus) came through resistance. He fought through other peoples' opinions. He fought through his own doubts, uncertainties and fears. When he got to Jesus, Jesus asked him, *"what do you want from me?"* His response was, "my sight." And in Mark 10:52 *"Jesus said to him, go your way; **your** faith has made you whole. And immediately he received his sight and followed Jesus in the way."* And on other occasions Jesus said something similar:

> *"According to **your** faith be it unto you."*
>
> *"As **you** have believed, be it unto you."*
>
> *"If **you** can believe, all things are possible to those who believe,"*

What are the Leading Causes of LIFE?

"***your*** faith has saved you." (Author emphasis)

Further, Paul writes in Ephesians 3:20, *"now unto him who is able to do exceeding abundantly above all that we ask or think according to the power that works in us."* **Everything God made has everything it needs to work.**

An appropriate affirmation for all humans is, **" I have the power!" " I have what it takes."**

In the world of Hollywood movie making, it is interesting to note that a skilled writer can use the same set of events to write different types of stories and thereby, create different movies. It's all a matter of emphasis. The same set of events, facts, figures, results can be used to write drama, horror, adventure, fiction, comedy, tragedy, triumph, victory or documentary. The difference is in the focus. The difference is in where the punctuation is placed. Comas, colons, semicolons, question marks, quotation marks, apostrophes, parenthesis, periods, exclamation points, dashes, hyphens and brackets all can change the meaning of a story. They can change the direction of a story. They can change the point of a story.

The Wayan brothers took the horror picture "Scream" and made a comedy called "Scary Movie." The same set of events that caused people to scream out of fear in the first movie, were manipulated such that they caused people to scream with laughter at the second movie. The difference

A Prescription of Living at Your Highest and Best

was in focus, emphasis and where the punctuation was placed.

Politics and politicians in America can be described as conservative and liberal. The difference between the two large categories is focus, emphasis and where they place punctuation. It's always interesting to note how there is one constitution on which the nation is founded and stands; Yet different people read the same document differently. Different people come to very different conclusions and make very different decisions after reading the same document.

The above examples, the US Constitution and movie making, serve as backdrop to the point. God is a god of wholeness. The universe is whole. Nature is whole. Humans are whole. Since the universe is whole, nature and humans are whole.

The universe, nature and humans have everything they need to work and since everything needed is present, the life we lead is a function of focus, emphasis and where the punctuation is placed.

You decide your life focus. You decide what you emphasize in life. You decide where the punctuation is placed in your life story. **Don't let others punctuate your life story. It's your story. Punctuate it!** Don't let people put a period where you want a comma. Don't allow exclamation points where only a period is necessary. Don't let someone else's colon replace your semicolon. Others' quotations should not substitute for yours. Use your own. Punctuate your own life.

What are the Leading Causes of LIFE?

We have within us the power to live our own life. We have within us everything needed to live a full and fruitful life. We are made whole. "Batteries are included." Nothing is missing. Everything needed to live life in abundance came preinstalled in the package. **How much life we live is a function of focus, emphasis and where the punctuation is placed.**

For example, in the human being, spirit is unlimited. Issues of the spirit get played out in our minds. Things like drive, determination, toughness, courage, faith, boldness, resilience are all issues of the spirit that are actualized in and through our minds. A specific example of this is the 'placebo response.' This is the body's biochemical and/or physiological reaction to a thought or belief that is firmly held by the mind. The belief creates biology. That is, the firmly held thought, meditation, prayer, belief, causes an accompanying chemical/physiological reaction. Indeed all thoughts are attached to a chemistry. Thoughts of joy create joy chemicals. Thoughts of sadness and sorrow create sadness and sorrow chemicals. Thoughts of healing create healing chemicals. Herein lies the essence of the placebo response. People who strongly believe they have been healed, produce healing chemicals that lead to facilitating the body's healing of itself.

All of this suggests that the human body, which was made whole and complete by God is designed to heal itself from within. The body just like nature, is designed to adapt, correct, compensate, redirect, resupply, regenerate or rebuild where necessary.

A brief look at other aspects of nature further indicates that everything God made has everything it needs to work.

Everything the sun needs to do what it does, it has within it. Imagine how much energy is being expended by the sun to provide light, heat, and energy to planet earth. The sun is 93,000,000 miles away, the exact distance necessary to provide the life giving, life supporting light, heat, and energy it provides to planet earth. The sun contains enough energy to travel 93,000,000 miles and then support life and give light to planet earth. This is an incredible reality. But, it reflects the wholeness or completeness of God.

Consider the redwood tree. It begins as a seed. Imagine, something the size of an object smaller than the tip of your smallest finger has within it the potential that is transformed into the largest living structure on earth. Redwood trees can grow to be 340-350 feet tall; 8-20 feet wide; they have bark that is one foot thick. One redwood tree can supply enough wood to build twenty-two houses. And so, in a real sense, a seed is unlimited in its potential. It only needs time and the right (nurturing) environment.

Seeds, in my view are one of the many great miracles (wonders) of nature. I continuously marvel at how God has placed so much in something so little. The wonder of the seed makes it clear to me that everything God made has everything it needs to work.

What are the Leading Causes of LIFE?

The seed is not only a tree, but also an orchard. In order for what is in the seed to be transformed into reality, the seed must be nourished. It must be placed in a stable, supportive, accepting, encouraging, and nourishing environment. **Any potential that is placed in a stable, supportive, accepting, encouraging, and nourishing environment will grow, develop and prosper.**

In the human condition, love creates an accepting, supportive, encouraging, nourishing and stable environment. So, children who are loved have the greatest chance of living life fully. **Love, then, can be called a leading cause of life.**

First John 4:16 says *"We know and rely on the love God has for us. God is love. Whoever lives in love lives in God, and God in them."* Since God is love, everything God made was made by love. What you love, you want to flourish. What you love, you want to live. What you love, you accept, give attention to, support, encourage, nourish and nurture. Love, then, supports life. Love enhances life. Love promotes life. **Love causes life.**

Love, like life, is whole. There is nothing halfway about love. Love reflects God. The wholeness of nature reflects God. The wholeness of life reflects God. Nature, including the life of humans, all emanate from the love of God. Love is built into humans. All humans have the capacity to love. It's built into us. This means all humans have the capacity to support, encourage, enhance, nourish, promote, nurture, indeed, cause life.

Where there is love, everything needed for life, health, healing and wholeness is present. Where there is love, nothing is missing. Where there is love, purpose is being fulfilled.

Love and wholeness track together. Wholeness and fulfillment of purpose track together. I often marvel at the sight of a tree bearing the fruit it was designed to produce. Only God could have invented the formula that takes a tiny seed and mixes it with soil and fecal matter to bring forth abundant fruit that will nourish and sustain for years to come. What God makes is complete. It's whole. It has everything it needs to work. From a seed, no bigger than a fraction of your fingernail, a tree is produced that may be several times larger than the average human. What is even more incredible is this tree can give you nourishment for the rest of your life. In a real sense, **the seed is unlimited in potential and capacity.** The seed has everything in it needed to fulfill its purpose. **The seed, when appropriately nourished, lives out its purpose, the ongoing provision of unlimited amounts of fruit.**

Similarly, humans come from something very small. At conception the two cells that come together forming an embryo are the size of a mere dot on this page. Over time, we grow, create, develop talents, ideas, inventions, and families that continue to nourish the world.

In the beginning God created the heavens and the earth, the whole picture, and it all had a designated purpose. God, the ultimate event planner, designated a purpose for the most magnificent part of his creation, mankind. Humans are His most precious seed. After all, we are made in His image. Genesis 1:26 *"Then God said, Let us make man in our image, after our likeness: and let them have dominion over the fish of the sea, and over the fowl of the air, and over the cattle, and over all the earth, and over every creeping thing that creep upon the earth."*

God is a god of love. **God is a god of wholeness. God does nothing halfway. God is always on purpose.** God has made us in his image. God made us whole. Wholeness and purpose track together. So, we were whole for a purpose, to be on that purpose.

From Genesis 1:1, *"In the beginning God created the heavens **and** the earth,"* (Author emphasis) we know that God is about the whole picture, the top and the bottom, inside and out, above and below. **God is all about the wholeness that brings into existence, makes things happen, the wholeness that is fruitful, and productive.** And so, from the beginning, God's purpose for our existence is to flourish, be fruitful and productive. This means, God placed within everything needed to achieve fruitfulness. In Genesis 1:28, God blessed man and told them to *"be fruitful..."* God didn't just create us for His amusement. He never does anything just to be doing it. He doesn't take opinion polls to see what we think about his plan and purpose.

Everything God does is deliberate, for a divine purpose, complete, and reflective of His love.

Because we are made in God's image, each of us is complete and whole. **Each of us has been given a unique purpose and fruit to bear.** And each of us has within us everything needed to make this happen.

Unfortunately, many of us fall short of fulfilling the purpose of bearing fruit. Rather than looking within self, too often we look elsewhere. Where people are unfulfilled, dissatisfied, and displeased with their lives, frequently they point blame, continuously complain, moan, and groan about unfairness in life. The problem is not the complaining, moaning and groaning. The problem is, this is all that is done. **Cursing darkness does not produce light.**

We gain insight into the mind of God through His word and work. Scripture is His word, nature is His work. His family is his work. We should study scripture and nature and His family for a closer look, a better understanding and a closer walk with God. A look at the wholeness and purpose that God intended for the tiny seed, for example, provides incredible insight and lessons for our own growth and development.

God's purpose for the seed is to become a tree that continuously bears fruit. Everything needed to become a tree is within the seed, but in order for the seed to become a tree it must give up being a seed. That is, the seed must die. It must be buried. It must be placed below ground level, covered with dirt, alone in the dark, shut off from other seeds.

In the human condition, to be fruitful we must go through a similar process. We must be willing to "die daily." We must be willing to give up being who we are and begin living out who God wants us to be. We must understand that people will treat you poorly; they will throw dirt on you, and try to bury your good name and deeds. Additionally, you will experience loneliness, darkness, and isolation.

It is a fascinating miracle of nature that a seed takes root and draws nourishment from the soil in which it is buried. **The dirt and soil in which it is buried becomes the foundation for the new life.**

Again, a similar thing occurs in the human condition. All the dirt, negative comments, criticisms, jealousies, fiery darts and gossip people try to bury you in can become the foundation on which you stand and in which you become rooted to have a more fulfilling and fruitful life. **Feces from one situation can serve as fertilizer for another.** What people mean to hurt you can be used to help you.

Genesis 50:20 is summarized by saying: what Joseph's brothers meant for evil against him, God helped Joseph to turn into good. There is a process then, through which a seed goes to achieve its purpose. It is the conversion or transformation process. First the husbandman or farmer digs a hole in the ground. Then, the seed is placed in that hole.

Next, the seed is covered by dirt and feces. Then the seed exists in the dark all alone. The journey begins below ground level. The seed must take root all by itself below ground level, in a pit. In order to be fruitful it must begin below ground level. The husbandman or farmer knows the precise location of the seeds and cares for and protects them as the process unfolds. The seed is nourished by the rain, the sun, and the nutrients in the soil.

In this, God created process. The seed uses the nutrient energy it receives from the rain, sun, and soil to take root and grow. **Like the seed, God knows where we are in our lives and can reach us even in the pits of life.** God challenges and inspires us to initiate the energy conversion/transformation process and to take the dirt, the isolation, and the criticism, and use it to nourish instead of diminish our lives. It is then that we take root and grow in our purpose and become fruitful.

As God's human seed, we often feel the pain of being buried in a pit. The pit is the place where people throw dirt on us; where they speak ill of us; it is where we are challenged; stretched and kicked; where we are fired from our jobs; where we have bad credit, bad relationships, bad health, and bad attitudes. It is in this pit that God stirs and talks to us. It is in the pit that God gets our attention sufficient for us to see better that he is purposing to produce fruit in and through us. It is in the pit, many times, that God perfects our faith in him.

So often the pains and trials we go through in life are so impacting, they not only prevent us from seeing but also from understanding that **there is purpose in pain.** Through faith the pain can be used as an inspiration to cause the growth that brings us out of our pits.

Understandably, people are afraid of life's pits. We do our best to avoid the problems and trials in life. **None of us seek problems and trials, but all of us must face them. How we face them determines what we get from them.** Learning to deal with pits, problems, challenges, changes, mountains, and valleys are what help us achieve purpose and bear fruit. **We must learn to be comfortable with being uncomfortable.** Where we are changes only through process.

We must have faith that God is directing our lives for his purpose. As we go out about our daily lives, God is working in ways we may not even notice.

So, know that:
- ✓ God stands in wellness and addresses our sickness
- ✓ He stands in joy and addresses our worry
- ✓ He stands in hope and addresses our hopelessness
- ✓ He stands in prosperity and addresses our poverty
- ✓ He stands in the way, truth, and life and addresses those who don't know which way to turn, and
- ✓ He stands in fruitfulness and addresses our bareness.

God is God of the whole story, the whole situation. God is a God of completeness. The fruit God is most concerned about is our perfected faith. When our faith is perfected our fruit is continuous and purposeful. With God we are something valuable and unique, purposeful and productive. If we try to live without him, we abandon the purpose for which we were made.

God's purpose in an acorn is to be a mighty oak tree. God's purpose in a caterpillar is to be a butterfly. God's purpose in a child is to be mature and a strong adult. God's purpose in us is to realize the ideas, thoughts, dreams, inventions, and imaginations he has placed in us!

Affirm today: I am here for a purpose! I am here for God's purpose. Affirm today that, **"God has for me a larger purpose! I will bear fruit!!"**

Bible verses relevant to your purpose:

1 John 3:8(b) For this purpose the Son of God was manifested that he might destroy the works of the devil.

Ecclesiastes 3:1 To everything there is a season, and a time to every purpose under heaven.

What are the Leading Causes of LIFE?

John 10:10 The thief comes to steal kill and destroy; I am come that you might have life in abundance.

Psalm 46:10 Be still and know that I am God; I will be exalted among the heaven and the earth.

Isaiah 55:8-11 For my thoughts are not your thoughts, neither are your ways my ways," declares the Lord.
[9] As the heavens are higher than the earth, so are my ways higher than your ways and my thoughts than your thoughts.
[10] As the rain and the snow come down from heaven,
and do not return to it without watering the earth
and making it bud and flourish, so that it yields seed for the sower and bread for the eater,
[11] so is my word that goes out from my mouth: It will not return to me empty, but will accomplish what I desire and achieve the purpose for which I sent it. that which I please, and it shall prosper in the thing where to I sent it.

Jeremiah 1:4-5 Then the word of the Lord came to me, saying, [5]Before I formed you in the womb I knew you, before you were born I set you apart; I appointed you as a prophet to the nations.

Isaiah. 46:3 Listen to me, you descendants of Jacob, all the remnant of the people of Israel, you whom I have upheld since your birth, and have carried since you were born.

Galatians.1:15 But when it pleased God, who separated me from my mother's womb, and called me by his grace.

People with a purpose have something to live for. Purpose empowers. Purpose energizes. Purpose enlivens. Purpose instructs. Purpose guides. Purpose directs. Purpose inspires. Purpose informs.

"Everything God made has everything it needs to work," is a "seed" statement. It is a "potential" statement. It is a "possibility" statement. It is a "power" statement.

A seed, potential, promise, possibility, and power all must experience an energy transfer to be fully realized. Energy must be transferred from other areas and applied to the seed, potential, promise, possibility and power for them to be fully achieved. Energy in the universe is constantly being converted from one form to another. **There is no "new" energy. There is converted energy.**

When energy is transferred from one area to another, the area in receipt of the energy is activated, fueled, enhanced, stimulated, empowered, and enlivened. What is energy? Energy is force. Energy is effective power. Energy is strength.

Energy is vigor. Energy is might. Energy is stimulation, animation, inspiration, and motivation. Energy is nourishment, nurturing, and fuel. Energy is focus, attention, and concentration. Energy fosters, urges, and encourages. Energy moves things and gets things going. Nature has energy. It has sufficient energy to keep going and going and going. **Nature is the ultimate example of the energizer bunny.**

The life of nature and its component parts results from its life supporting, life sustaining, life strengthening, life growing, life developing, and life restoring energy.

A wonderful example of how everything God made has everything it needs to work is the butterfly. The butterfly begins as an egg. Then it hatches into the larva stage or caterpillar. The caterpillar then forms a cocoon to separate itself from the outside world and accomplish the final stage of its conversion into a butterfly. The caterpillar worm, inside the cocoon, initiates a process whereby its organs actually melt down and are reconstructed/reconstituted as organs necessary to support a new and flying creature. The organs of a caterpillar worm (larva stage) support a slithering, slow moving, constantly eating, and non-productive, and extremely limited creature.

Before a butterfly can emerge from the cocoon, the caterpillar must be converted/transformed. It is transformed from the inside. New organs and support structures are necessary and formed to support a flying, quick moving, highly productive and almost unlimited creature.

What is amazing to me is **the butterfly is in the caterpillar worm. The caterpillar worm has everything it needs in it to become a butterfly.** Through a conversion/transformation process occurring in stages, from an egg comes a caterpillar worm. From a caterpillar worm comes a cocoon. From the cocoon comes a butterfly.

This amazing conversion/transformation process is characteristic of nature. **Lower level existence is transformed to higher levels through the transfer or exchange of energy.** No new energy is created. There is a shift in focus of already existing energy such that something new is brought forth out of the old situation.

Everything that a fertilized human egg can grow and develop into is present at the moment of conception. When one of the three hundred million sperm in a healthy ejaculate reaches and fertilizes an egg, the one cell that is formed is the size of a dot on this piece of paper. From that one cell dot will come a fully developed human being comprised of many different tissues, organs, structures, and systems totaling somewhere in the neighborhood of 75 to 100 trillion cells. Incredible! **God does nothing half way.** Whatever God makes is whole, complete, thorough, and therefore has all/everything it needs to work.

What are the Leading Causes of LIFE?

Before there was writing, before there were books, before there were classrooms, laboratories or schools, there was the work of God. There was the work of nature. Human beings are a part of nature. From our very beginning we have been on a quest to understand the meaning of nature and life and how humans fit into the whole picture. The search for this meaning revolves around the intersection of scripture and science, ministry and medicine, spirituality and health.

Nature is the primary place where spirituality and science intersect. Both spirituality and science emerge from nature, have nature as their source of inspiration and information, and are similar in that divine revelation and scientific discovery could be described as the same thing.

In the human condition, there is a constant, complex, interconnected, interdependent, interplay between our spirit, mind and body. The "whole" human being has a tripartite existence, spirit, mind and body. The whole human being has everything needed to work. The whole human being has the power and authority to transfer/shift/exchange energy from one portion of its existence to another. That is, our spiritual energy can be applied to our mind or body or our mental (intellectual and emotional) energy can be applied to our body, or our physical (body) energy can be used to grow and develop mental and/or spiritual strength. **Humans function at their highest and best when utilizing their whole being and leading with their strongest component, the spirit.**

This wholistic perspective is not new. The recognition of the human condition as one of spirit, mind, and body is as old as humans themselves. Thousands of years ago in ancient Africa, the birthplace of all humans there was recognition of the tripartite (spirit, mind, body) nature of the human being. Dr. Charles Finch in his book *The African Background to Medical Science* (1990), published by Karnak house, states:

> "Egyptian physicians were trained in the 'per ankh' or 'house of life' which served as a university, library, medical school, clinic, temple and seminary....in these centers of learning there was no sharp demarcation between the fields of study; religion, philosophy, science, astronomy, mathematics, music and hieroglyphics were all part of the same species of knowledge and were reflected in one another."

Life is whole. All of life is lived at the same time. How much of it we engage or experience or utilize is another matter. This says to me, **the capacity for a full life, a whole life, a complete life, an accomplished life, a life of significance and substance, is present in *all* humans**. In fact, it came preinstalled in the package.

Of all people, Jesus was clear about this first law of thermodynamics. He established it and put it in motion in the first place. He has firsthand knowledge of what is placed in everything to make it work. He made it. John 1:1-3, *"In the beginning was the Word and the Word was with God and the Word was God. All things were made by him, and without him was not anything made that was made."*

Jesus always worked with what he had to get what he wanted. He knew people could always do better and more. He knew because he built better and more into them. And so, an important, if not the most important, focus of Jesus' ministry was empowerment. **Jesus always moved people, challenged people to achieve their full potential. He charged people to their highest and best.** Jesus was the antithesis to disease, distress, disorder, and doubt.

To people who were diseased, he brought peace, wholeness, completeness, and healing.

To people who were distressed he brought calm assurance.

To people whose lives were in disorder and disarray he brought order and alignment.

To people who were in doubt he brought faith and certainty.

Jesus, in his ministry of empowerment, was successful in getting people to transfer and convert their energy from one life area and form to another. He inspired people to tap into their power within. **Healing and wholeness come from within.** That's where God preinstalled it when he made us.

A modern day display of the power within is the story of what has come to be called the "Central Park Jogger." This story is about a young lady in her late twenties, 28, a graduate of Yale University, very smart (Phi Beta Kappa), on the executive fast track at the investment-banking firm of Salomon Brothers. One day while jogging she was attacked, raped, and brutally beaten to the point where most people, including medical experts, thought she would certainly die. She remained in a coma for twelve days. She suffered cuts, gashes bone fractures, an eye socket with multiple fractures, severe blood loss, and brain damage. She could not breathe on her own. And there were those who felt it would be better for her if she died. She did not die. She lived!

The resilience she manifested in her amazing recovery came from within her. According to a June 29, 2005, USA Today article - page 20, her recovery is consistent with recent research findings on overcoming severe trauma and other major difficulties. The article identified and summarized some of the findings important to overcoming trauma or being resilient:

- Optimism with an attitude of *"I can do this"*
- An emphasis on the "now", stay in the "present"
- Courage. Face the challenge. Don't hide from it.
- Connect with others and accept their help
- Be spiritual. Understand, there is a higher power.

We are not here alone, nor are we here to be alone. We are here for each other. Sixteen years after the life threatening traumatic event which left her in a coma and not expected to live, she, Trisha

Meili, returned to Salomon Brothers, achieved the vice presidency she always wanted, felt there was more to life, moved on from investment banking, and started a new career in motivational speaking designed to help people be resilient. She managed the hard work of energy transfer and conversion. The healing and restoration experienced by Trisha Meili came from within her. Just as nature has the power to heal and restore itself, so do humans. This power is built in, but, not always tapped into and realized.

Oliver Wendell Holmes once said, "What lies ahead of us and what lies behind us are tiny matters compared to what lies within us."

When God asked Moses *"what's in your hand?"*, (Exodus 4:2), it was a question designed to get Moses to appreciate that everything he needed to do all that God required of him, he already had it. He had the power. The power was within him. The first law of thermodynamics should instruct and inspire us to first look within, notice, and fully appreciate and value who you are with all of your gifts and talents.

Everything needed to succeed in life, we have within us. It's a matter of making a decision to tap into the power within. It should be noticed that, in the Bible, **God always speaks directly to the one or ones in difficulty.** God speaks directly to those in pain, in fear, in hiding, in hunger, in prison, in sickness, in sorrow, in death and challenges them to tap into the power within and those who made the decision to comply with the Word of God always achieved victory.

God first calls on the one directly affected. God speaks directly to the disabled, disempowered, discouraged, diseased, distressed, disillusioned and depressed. God speaks to that power He knows is within us. God knows it because He placed it there.

Those who seriously seek spiritual strength are always successful. Those who prioritize their spiritual life always find strength to move beyond where they are, and closer to, if not to, where they want to be. This point is emphasized in scripture by the following:

> I Samuel 17:33-37, 44-47 (NIV-Life Application):
> *^{33} Saul replied, "You are not able to go out against this Philistine and fight him; you are only a boy, and he has been a fighting man from his youth." ^{34} But David said to Saul, "Your servant has been keeping his father's sheep. When a lion or a bear came and carried off a sheep from the flock, ^{35} I went after it, struck it and rescued the sheep from its mouth and killed it. ^{36} Your servant has killed both the lion and the bear; this uncircumcised Philistine will be like one of them, because he has defied the armies of the living God."*
> *^{37}The Lord who delivered me from the paw of the lion and the paw of the bear will deliver me from the hand of this Philistine."*
> *^{44}"Come here," he said, "and I'll give your flesh to the birds of the air and the beasts of*

What are the Leading Causes of LIFE?

> *the field!" ⁴⁵David said to the Philistine, "You come against me with sword and spear and javelin, but I come against you in the name of the Lord Almighty, the God of the armies of Israel, whom you have defied. ⁴⁶This day the Lord will hand you over to me, and I'll strike you down and cut off your head. Today I will give the carcasses of the Philistine army to the birds of the air and the beasts of the earth, and the whole world will know that there is a God in Israel. ⁴⁷All those gathered here will know that it is not by sword or spear that the Lord saves; for the battle is the Lord's, and he will give all of you into our hands."*

A message I get from this passage of scripture is superior talent and no spirit cannot defeat average talent and superior spirit. It is in the realm of the spirit that we find things like drive, determination, desire, discipline, resolve, resilience, patience, and persistence. If all you are depending on is talent, you are not taking advantage of all that is available to you, and, you will never be all that you can be.

Learn to tap into and depend on your spiritual self. Your spirit is the strongest part of you. **Your spirit is unlimited. Your spirit is your true life force.** The more you tap into and depend on your spiritual self, the more life you will experience. This includes, of course, the fact that you will do more and bigger things in life.

Goliath had superior talent and inferior spirit. David had inferior talent and superior spirit. David was more successful than Goliath. David lived a larger life than Goliath. David lived a deeper, wider, and higher level life than Goliath. David trusted and depended on his source of life. He depended on God for his success, not his talent ability. Whatever your talent ability level, it is never more important than your spiritual self. Your success in life is more a function of where and how strong your spirit is, than how much talent ability you have.

I am not discounting or dismissing the importance of and contribution of talent ability. It can and does make a powerful difference, but talent ability levels differ from person to person. Different people are gifted in different ways at different levels. This is one of the beauties of God's garden. Like flowers, different humans are beautiful and beautifully gifted in different ways, but the great equalizer, which is equally available to all of us, is the spirit of God. To the degree you tap into that part of you that is unlimited, you grow yourself, strength and power to match the Goliath you are facing. In the face of superior talent develop superior spirit. Superior spirit guarantees more life. It guarantees greater life. It guarantees more and greater success in life.

Imagine just for a moment, a superior talent ability and superior spirit combination. Sounds like Jesus doesn't it? Superior spirit will drive you to develop your talent ability to its highest and best, and it can make up for what you lack in talent ability.

Samuel 23:2-4, 7-12 (NIV-Life Application):
> ² **He inquired of the Lord, saying,** *"Shall I go and attack these Philistines?"* ³*But David's men said to him, "Here in Judah we are afraid. How much more, then, if we go to Keilah against the Philistine forces!"*
> ⁴ **Once again David inquired of the Lord,** *and the Lord answered him, "Go down to Keilah, for I am going to give the Philistines into your hand,* ⁵*So David and his men went to Keilah, fought the Philistines and carried off their livestock. He inflicted heavy losses on the Philistines and saved the people of Keilah.*

2 Samuel 5:19, 23 (NIV-Life Application):
> ¹⁹**So David inquired of the Lord,** *"Shall I go and attack the Philistines? Will you hand them over to me?"*
>
> ²³**So David inquired of the Lord,** *and he answered, "Do not go straight up, but circle around behind them and attack them in front of the balsam trees."*

(Author emphasis)

In every instance where David puts God first, prioritizes his spiritual life and strength, he is always successful. **The strongest part of the human condition is the spirit.** The part of the human being that has the most to be called on is the spirit. The part of the human being where too often too much of it goes untapped is the spirit. The part of the human being that is available for great challenges that exceed our physical abilities is the spirit.

The spirit is the life strength and force that enables us to press forward. It is the push that says, keep going. It is the inspiration and motivation that says, it can be done and further, you can do it. Spirit is within us and available to us. Spirit came preinstalled in the human being package for general use and for use during serious adversity. **Spirit is the part of the human being that is unlimited, unafraid and unconditional. The spirit is a part of us placed in us by God to enable us to do everything we need to do to work.**

> 2 Corinthians 3:17 (NIV-Life Application):
> *Now the Lord is the Spirit, and where the Spirit of the Lord is, there is freedom.*

Spiritual strength is what makes it possible for it to be said about human beings that everything God made has everything it needs to work. What humans lack in artistic talent can be compensated for through spiritual strength. Barriers, no matter how big or bad can be broken by tapping into your

spiritual strength. Whatever binds you can be broken by the Spirit of God.
God is unlimited. Spirit is unlimited. God has no limits. Spirit has no limits.

> 2 Timothy 1:7 (NIV-Life Application):
> *For God has not given us a spirit of fear, but of power, love and a sound mind.*

The spirit placed in us by God is unlimited and unafraid in all conditions. Spirit always indicates what should be done that it can be done, and you can do it.

> Judges 6:1-16 (NIV-Life Application):
> *¹Again the Israelites did evil in the eyes of the Lord, and for seven years he gave them into the hands of the Midianites. ²Because the power of Midian was so oppressive, the Israelites prepared shelters for themselves in mountain clefts, caves and strongholds.*
> *³Whenever the Israelites planted their crops, the Midianites, Amalekites and other eastern peoples invaded the Country. ⁴They camped on the land and ruined the crops all the way to Gaza and did not spare a living thing for Israel, neither sheep nor cattle nor donkeys. ⁵They came up with their livestock and their tents like swarms of locusts. It was impossible to count the men and their camels; they invaded the land to ravage it. ⁶Midian so impoverished the Israelites that they cried out to the Lord for help. ⁷When*

the Israelites cried to the Lord because of Midian, ^{8}He sent them a prophet, who said, "This is what the Lord, the God of Israel says: I brought you up out of Egypt, out of the land of slavery. ^{9} snatched you from the power of Egypt and from the hand of all your oppressors. I drove them from before you and gave you their land. ^{10}I said to you, 'But you have not listened to me.'"

^{11}The angel of the Lord came and sat down under the oak in Ophrah that belonged to Joash the Abiezrite, where his son Gideon was threshing wheat in a winepress to keep it from the Midianites. ^{12}When the angel of the Lord appeared to Gideon, he said, "The Lord is with you, mighty warrior." ^{13}"But sir," Gideon replied, "if the Lord is with me, why has all this happened to us? Where are all his wonders that our fathers told us about when they said, 'Did not the Lord bring us up out of Egypt?' But now the Lord has abandoned us and put us into the hand of Midian." ^{14}The Lord turned to him and said, "Go in the strength you have and save Israel out of Midian's hand. Am I not sending you?" ^{15}"But Lord" Gideon asked, "how can I save Israel? My clan is the weakest in Manasseh, and I am the least in my family." ^{16}The Lord answered, "I will be with you, and you will strike down all the Midianites together."

What are the Leading Causes of LIFE?

When God gives direction, He is simultaneously saying it can be done and, you can do it. In other words, you have everything you need to do what is placed before you, challenging you.

God's direction can always be recognized by the fact that it moves towards abundant life. **God's direction is always towards life for everyone.** Those directly involved and those indirectly involved but close enough to be affected will be impacted by the life God's spirit brings.

God's spirit is unlimited. God's spirit is liberating. The more you tap into the spirit of God, the more liberated and unlimited you become.

Often times the shackles or limits that we need to be liberated from are internal. That is, we place limits on what we think is possible. We place limits on what we think can be done and on what we think we can do. **Self-imposed limits are very difficult to be liberated from,** but our spirit knows no limits. And spiritually when we determine to do something it gets done.

Spiritually, all humans operate on a level playing field. Physical abilities are different, but we all have access to the same spirit. We can all tap into spiritual power. Since spiritual power is unlimited, we can utilize as much as is needed to accomplish whatever is needed. The realm of the spirit is the great equalizer. People with less talent and natural physical ability can compensate by tapping into their spiritual power, which is limitless. This is the story of the Bible. Facing odds greater than themselves people tapped into their spiritual power, withdrew and utilized all they needed to successfully handle the challenge. Probably the most quoted of such Biblical examples is the confrontation between David and Goliath.

When facing natural and physical odds that are overwhelming, remember, spiritual power can compensate. Desire, drive, determination have more to do with success in life than natural ability. How much you want something and how hard you're willing to work at it, are the issues/questions that are more likely to result in success than natural ability. These questions deal with capacity.

Human beings have unlimited capacity. Humans have unlimited content. Humans have unlimited aptitude. Humans have unlimited potential. Humans are unlimited. Made in the image of God humans are unlimited.

Capacity is built into us. The capacity built into us is dynamic. It does not remain static. It is alive. It can be grown and developed. Education, training, information, knowledge, wisdom, insight, imagination all enhance capacity, and thereby life. People who take the time and make the effort can learn new skills, develop new abilities, assume new habits. These **new skills, new abilities, new habits represent new life. They represent more life. They represent expanded capacity. This means, of course that people who decide to continue their**

education, continue to grow their capacity, and thereby, they enhance their life. Further, education, continuous learning, and training, are always available at some level to everybody.
A magnificent expression of this truth is a man called Tony Melendez. His story was capsulized in a Newark New Jersey Star Ledger newspaper article on page one of the 'In The Towns' section, on February 2, 2006. This article described how Mr. Melendez was born with no arms. His mother was prescribed thalidomide to help alleviate the morning sickness associated with pregnancy. Thalidomide caused the genetic malfunction and malformation of baby Melendez that resulted in the absence of upper extremities.

Yet, despite having no arms, Mr. Melendez had the desire, drive and determination to play the guitar. The guitar, as everybody knows, is an instrument requiring the use of both hands. Mr. Melendez had no hands but he did have desire, drive and determination. Because of these spiritual qualities, he was able to compensate for the lack of arms. He tapped into his spiritual power to overcome the low self-esteem, ridicule, physical hardship, feeling sorry for himself and extra time needed to handle even simple tasks. He overcame these challenges and learned to play the guitar with his feet. Mr. Melendez is the rhythm guitar player and lead singer for his band called Toe Jam. At the writing of the article, they had toured thirty-three countries, produced seven albums and played before the Pope five times. The message he brings to people in word and performance is, "never give up on life." Tony Melendez is just one example of the principle, **"Everything made by God has everything it needs to work."**

The spirit of the human being is unlimited. The true capacity of the human being resides in the spirit. Therefore human capacity is really unlimited. Human beings can really do whatever they decide to do. The issue/challenge is, deciding. The issue/challenge is, the will. The issue/challenge is, desire, drive, determination. The issue/challenge is, fire to start, fuel to sustain and fight to succeed. Achievement results from the fire to start, fuel to sustain and fight to succeed.

Fire, fuel and fight reside in the realm of the spirit. They are capacity qualities. They are available to all regardless of natural talent or ability. The apostle Paul made reference to this point at the end of his life when he wrote in 2nd Timothy 4:6-7, *"For I am now ready to be offered, and the time of my departure is at hand. I have fought a good fight, I have finished my course, I have kept the faith."* Everything Paul did came from within him. He had within him everything he needed to do, everything he wanted to do or that God asked him to do. As is true with all of us, Paul either had the capacity or used his capacity to grow and develop additional capacity to meet the challenge. In either case, he had everything needed to do the work he wanted and needed to do.

Harriet Tubman is another excellent example of a person who had extremely limited natural, physical ability but compensated for that by tapping into the spiritual reserves placed within her by God. God gave her everything needed to do whatever she was inspired to do.

Ms. Tubman was born a slave. She could neither read nor write. At an early age she was hit in the head with an iron weight thrown by a slave master. From that point she experienced a condition called narcolepsy. It caused her to uncontrollably fall asleep. Sometimes in mid-sentence she would fall asleep. This led to her being ridiculed by siblings and other slaves. Combined with what many would today describe as being esthetically challenged, her narcolepsy made many call her "slow." Certainly things were more difficult for her than her other "more normal" siblings. Ms. Tubman was nicknamed "Ugly Hat."

Yet despite her physical and intellectual limitations she achieved greatness. She did work that not only distinguished her, but established her as one of the great heroines who helped shape the destiny of this country.

If Harriet Tubman did her work in the arena of tennis, she would be the equivalent of Venus and Serena Williams, Arthur Ashe and Althea Gibson combined. If Harriet Tubman did her work in the arena of boxing she would be the equivalent of Muhammad Ali, Joe Louis and Jack Johnson combined. If Harriet Tubman had done her work in the area of politics, she would be the equivalent of Ralph Bunch, Colin Powell and Condoleezza Rice combined. If Harriet Tubman had done her work in the area of music she would have been the equivalent of Marian Anderson, Mahalia Jackson,

Aretha Franklin and Gladys Knight combined. Harriet Tubman was not any of these great achievers but what she did helped make all of what they did possible.

Imagine, a poor, esthetically challenged, "mentally slow," black slave woman managed to tap into the spiritual power placed in her by God and achieved greatness of historical magnitude.

Harriet Tubman escaped slavery herself. Then, not satisfied, she returned to the south on nineteen additional occasions to help approximately 1,000 slaves escape to freedom – from *Harriet Tubman: The Moses of Her People* by Sara Bradford, 1897. She learned to read and use the signs of nature, to help her determine direction. She learned to deal effectively and efficiently with people as there was no room for error in her work. She learned to trust her instincts. She learned to trust her intelligence. She learned to trust her imagination. She learned to trust her intuition. In other words, and mostly, **she learned to trust God**.

Her biography describes an incident where she was on a train that was stopped by authorities looking for her. They began a car-by-car search of the train. Ms. Tubman knew that it was common knowledge that she could not read. As the authorities approached her car, she picked up a newspaper. When the authorities reached her seat, she was holding the newspaper with both hands and focusing and scanning it just like she had seen people do who knew how to read. The authorities, noticing her "reading" kept moving through the train. Ms Tubman said, when the officials reached her seat, her prayer to God was, *"Lord, please let this newspaper be right side up."* Her prayer was answered.

Harriet Tubman became known as the conductor on the Underground Railroad. She became responsible for conducting more slaves to freedom than any other single person. And she is additionally famous for not ever losing a passenger. At one point there was a $40,000 reward posted for her capture (reference cited above). But, tapping into what God made available to her, she was able to achieve a success worthy of historical note. Harriet Tubman lived as if she knew that **"everything God made has everything it needs to work."**

Chapter 4
*Everything God Made **Was Made To Do Work***

The 2nd law of thermodynamics says: there is a universal tendency for order to break down into disorder unless counteracted by work. This is known as the law of entropy.

Work is necessary to maintain order. **God is a god of order. Work is necessary to maintain order.** So, this means God is also a god of work. Everything God made was made to do work. Work is the systematic application of energy. Work keeps the universe going. Work keeps nature going. In fact, work keeps everything going. Without work things stop. The reason anything stops that was going is, that work stopped.

Work is effort. It is systematic effort that is applied towards a specific purpose. The effort of work is required to overcome the resistance of the status quo. Things don't move, go or grow automatically. An expenditure of energy is necessary. This expenditure of energy is known as work. **Everything God made was made to do work.**

The work plan of God's creation is built into each part. The structure of each part is specifically designed to meet its work plan:
- The heart is designed for its pumping function.

What are the Leading Causes of LIFE?

- Lungs are designed for their breathing, exchange of carbon dioxide for oxygen function.
- The gastrointestinal system was designed for its nutrition retention and waste elimination functions.
- The muscular skeletal system was designed for its movement that allows for the contact that occurs as a result of the interfacing and interacting with the natural environment.
- Eyes are structured to do the work of vision and ears the work of hearing.
- The central nervous system is designed to do the work of sensing, thinking, feeling, and responding.

External to the human being the pattern is the same. **Every part of nature is structured to meet its work plan.** The sun, the moon, the rivers, the oceans, the trees, vegetation, the mountains, the soil, the birds, the bees, the butterflies, the plankton, the minnows, the turtles, the sharks, the whales, the insects, the bacteria, the clouds, the winds, the crops, the livestock are all structured to meet the work plan built into them by God.

All of nature does work, and it does its work perfectly. Life itself is dependent on every part of nature doing the work it was made to do. Because the sun does the work it is designed to do, life is sustained. Because the rivers, streams, and oceans do what they are designed to do, life is sustained. Because trees and vegetation do what they were designed to do life is sustained.

All of the rules/tasks/purposes outlined by God for man in Genesis 1:28 involve work. The exercise of authority, being productive, multiplying (change, creativity), replenishing (giving back, nurturing), managing (monitoring, maintaining) are all process that involve work (expenditure of energy).

Further, Genesis 2:15 outlines the first work command given in the Bible. It explains that man was placed in the garden of Eden, (delight) to "dress and keep" it. Work must be done to make a garden and keep a garden. Without work a garden becomes a jungle. A jungle is a place where anything grows and anything goes. This is my definition. A jungle is an absence of order. A jungle is an absence of the work necessary to achieve order.

Every part of nature has a work assignment. Nothing in nature is superfluous. Everything in nature does its work assignment. In fact, the **only** work done by the various pieces of nature is the work necessary to achieve their contribution to the overall plan, life. **Work is a basic ingredient of life. Work is required for life. There can be no life without work.** The growth, development, maintenance, sustenance, and adjustments of life require work. **To bring things into existence requires work. To make things happen requires work. To achieve full potential requires work.** To make progress requires work. To build requires work. **Work is an essential ingredient to life.** Everything worthwhile must be worked at to be fully realized and appreciated. For example, anything that contributes to life requires the systematic application of energy, work. Health and fitness require work. Relationship requires work. Love requires work. Faith requires work. Kindness, righteousness, humility, and self-discipline require work. Everything that contributes to life and its enhancement requires work. **Everything valuable to the maximization of life requires work.**

If you want a garden you have to work at it. If you want to build something you must work at it. If you want to achieve health, fitness, the honor roll, a successful relationship, starting a business, you must work at them. True life requires the expenditure of effort and energy. If you want to make something happen you must work at it. When you want to make something happen you must work at it. Life and work track together.

The case could be made that life is work, and work is life. That, that is alive must work, and **work is an indication of life.** Nature teaches us that you don't get something for nothing, no matter what it is. Everything comes with an attached energy/effort price.

Work is the price paid for accomplishment. Nothing is accomplished without the energy/effort of work. Learning a language, learning an instrument, pursuing a degree, maintaining a house, cleaning a room, establishing and operating a business or an organization, shopping, cooking, washing, studying, painting, practicing, raising children all require the energy-effort expenditure called work.

An explosion is disorganized or unorganized energy. Work is organized energy. Work is energy directed. An explosion is energy undirected.

The Bible makes many references to work and its connection with and importance to life. For example, James 2:17 says, *"Faith without works is dead."* Faith is essential to life. However, faith is intangible. To have any significance in this life, faith must be translated into tangible acts, deeds, behavior, or work. **Faith is the spiritual principle that underpins work. Faith and work are two sides of the same coin. Faith not acted on, or not worked at, is not faith.** Faith at its perfect best is behavior or work. *"Faith is the substance of things hoped for, the evidence of things not seen"* Heb. 11:1. Faith is "substance and evidence." Substance and evidence are work. **All work then is the substance and evidence of life,** because we live by faith.

If you're not working at life you're not living, you're just existing. **Life is work.** Life is the systematic application of energy around a specific purpose. **Work accomplishes.**

The accomplishments of work engenders joy. **The goal of work is accomplishment. The result of accomplishment is joy.** And so, **just as work and life track together, so**

do work and joy track together and if work and joy track together, so do life and joy.

The joy that results from the successful accomplishment of goals can be said to be what life is all about. The successful accomplishment of goals can only occur through work. Everything made by God was made to do work.

Life emerges through work. Things are brought into existence through work. Things are brought to life through work. People are brought to life through work. Only "nothing" happens without work. Work makes a difference. Work makes a difference between existence and non- existence. The formula is quite simple, non-existence + work (which includes a plan) = existence.

For example, the difference between a jungle and a garden is a plan plus work. The difference between noise and music is a plan plus work. The difference between a pile of concrete and steel and a skyscraper is a plan plus work. The difference between dating and marriage is a plan plus work. The difference between average and failing grades and academic excellence is a plan plus work. The difference between poverty and prosperity is a plan plus work.

All of nature works, following a built in plan that guarantees successful accomplishment of its assigned work purpose.

Humans, according to scripture, have a specific work assignment. **We are here to exercise dominion.** That is, to be in charge of the earth. We are here to manage and maintain the earth. We are here to monitor the earth. We are here to grow, develop, and maximize the earth. We are here to produce, protect, provide for and prosper life on earth.

This work purpose begins with ourselves. And it begins with the most important part of ourselves, the spiritual part. **Work is necessary to build anything.** Anything that is built is built to do work and it is the appropriate doing of that work that actually enhances the life of the thing. And so, when we do spiritual work we enhance our spiritual lives. When we expend spiritual energy and accomplish spiritual goals, we experience spiritual joy.

I believe that the reason everything God made was made to do work is, **work and joy track together**. God wants us to have joy in our work lives. God wants us to work. God wants us to move forward as a result of the work we do. God wants us to accomplish. God wants us to experience the joy that accompanies accomplishment. The successful accomplishment of a work goal, especially against serious odds, brings joy.

Further, joy strengthens. Joy inspires. Joy motivates. Joy makes you want more in life. Joy energizes you to do more work. Nehemiah 8:10 says, *"Go and enjoy choice food and sweet drinks, and send some to those who have nothing prepared. This day is sacred to our Lord. Do not grieve, for the joy of the Lord is your strength."* This experience of joy occurred as a result of the accomplishment of the work goal of rebuilding the walls of Jerusalem and it was accomplished against serious odds, external and internal.

The birth of a baby is a joyous occasion. This is so because of the labor/work associated with its accomplishment. John 16:21 says *"A woman giving birth to a child has pain because her time has come; but when her baby is born she forgets anguish because of her joy that a child is born into the world."* Women who give birth described labor as pain far surpassing any other pains they've experienced. Indeed the pains are so great that it is quite common for women to declare they will never have another baby. Some even described the labor/work pains as being indescribable. It is the joy of accomplishing a new birth that strengthens the person to try it again.

Serious, challenging, life changing work inspires joy when its accomplished. It also generates joy along the way. **Serious life work provides joy in the journey.** Hebrew 12:2 says this about Jesus and the serious work he was doing, *"Let us fix your eyes on Jesus, the author and perfecter of our faith, who for the joy set before him endured the cross, scorning its shame, and sat down at the right hand of the throne of God."*

The hardest work humans do is spiritual work. The greatest joy we experience in life results from spiritual work. This leads me to the conclusion, the most important work we do in life is, work directed at others. **Work designed to enhance the life, health, and well-being of others is the most important work one**

can do. Why? It causes life! It enhances the life of the one who is targeted, and it inspires the life of the one who is doing it. This is why spiritual work is so rewarding. Doing spiritual work (work targeted at improving the health, healing and well-being of others) is life giving. The lives of the give-ee and the give-er are both enhanced.

Consider the times when you have helped people who couldn't help themselves, or were kind to people who just needed an encouraging word, or provided the assistance that people tried to but couldn't find anywhere else, or paid attention to someone ignored and overlooked by everybody else. These times, especially when fully appreciated, but even when they are not, provide the kind of fulfillment and joy unmatched by other kinds of work. **Work that is "other" centered is the kind of work that adds life to our years and years to our life.**

People who have determined their purpose in life are enthusiastic about working that purpose. People who have identified their "life's" work are excited and energized when doing it. People who have found what they are clear is their purpose, mission, reason for being on this earth, willingly work hard at it and are always fulfilled by it.

Mark 3:31-35 says, *"Then Jesus' mother and brothers arrived. Standing outside, they sent someone in to call him. ^{32}A crowd was sitting around him, and they told him, 'Your mother and brothers are outside looking for you.' ^{33}'Who are* *my mother and brothers?' he asked.* ³⁴*Then he looked at those seated in a circle around him and said, 'Here are my mother and my brothers!* ³⁵*Whoever does God's will is my brother and sister and mother.'"*

This passage of scripture describes a situation where the biological family of Jesus were seriously concerned about how hard and long Jesus was working. They wanted to rescue him and give him an opportunity to get some rest. But Jesus pointed out to them and the others, gathered that he was doing the work (spiritual work; work designed to enhance the well-being of others) He came to do. This work was His purpose, His mission, and His reason for being on earth. This work was His highest priority. He had to do it. He was compelled to do it. He was driven to do it. The work God placed in you to do calls you, pulls you, pushes you, drives you, inspires you, motivates you, and energizes you.

Jeremiah had this experience. Because of the difficulty caused by his life's work, Jeremiah wanted to and determined that he would quit. But, your life's work, purpose, and mission will not leave you alone. Jeremiah 20:7-9 says, *"O Lord, you deceived me, and I was deceived; you overpowered me and prevailed. I am ridiculed all day long; everyone mocks me.* ⁸*Whenever I speak, I cry out proclaiming violence and destruction. So the word of the Lord has brought me insult and reproach all day long.* ⁹*But if I say I will not mention him or speak any more in His name, His word is in my heart like fire, a fire shut up in my* bones. I am weary of holding it in; indeed, I cannot."

Elijah had a similar experience. Your life's work, purpose, and mission will not leave you alone. It will keep calling you, keep talking to you, keep pulling at you, and keep driving you. I Kings 19:1-16 says: (NIV-Life Application)

> Now Ahab told Jezebel everything Elijah had done and how he had killed all the prophets with the sword. ²So Jezebel sent a messenger to Elijah to say, "May the gods deal with me, be it ever so severely, if by this time tomorrow I do not make your life like that of one of them." ³Elijah was afraid and ran for his life. When he came to Beersheba in Judah, he left his servant there, ⁴while he himself went a day's journey into the desert.
>
> He came to a broom tree, sat down under it and prayed that he might die. "I have had enough, Lord," he said. "Take my life; I am no better than my ancestors."
>
> ⁵Then he lay down under the tree and fell asleep. All at once an angel touched him and said, "Get up and eat." ⁶He looked around, and there by his head was a cake of bread baked over hot coals, and a jar of water. He ate and drank and then lay down again. ⁷The angel of the Lord came back a second time and touched him and said, "Get up and eat, for the journey is too much for

you." ⁸*So he got up and ate and drank. Strengthened by that food, he traveled forty days and forty nights until he reached Horeb, the mountain of God.*

⁹*There he went into a cave and spent the night and the word of the Lord came to him: "What are you doing here, Elijah?"*

¹⁰*He replied, "I have been very zealous for the Lord God Almighty. The Israelites have rejected your covenant, broken down your altars, and put your prophets to death with the sword. I am the only one left, and now they are trying to kill me too."*

¹¹*The Lord said, "Go out and stand on the mountain in the presence of the Lord, for the Lord is about to pass by." Then a great and powerful wind tore the mountains apart and shattered the rocks before the Lord, but the Lord was not in the wind. After the wind there was an earthquake, but the Lord was not in the earthquake.* ¹²*After the earthquake came a fire, but the Lord was not in fire, and after the fire came a gentle whisper.*

¹³*When Elijah heard it, he pulled his cloak over his face and went out and stood at the mouth of the cave. Then a voice said to him, "What are you doing here, Elijah?"*

> ^{14}He replied, "I have been very zealous for the Lord God Almighty. The Israelites have the sword. I am the only one left, and now they are trying to kill me too."
>
> ^{15}The Lord said to him, "Go back the way you came, and go to the Desert of Damascus. When you get there anoint Hazael, king over Aram. ^{16}Also, anoint Jehu, son of Nimshi king over Israel, and anoint Elisha, son of Shaphat from Abel Meholah, to succeed you as prophet."

God would not leave Elijah alone. As afraid as Elijah was about continuing and as much as he wanted to back away from his God given work assignment, God would not leave him alone.

Work that is other centered, is the most important work we do. It's often difficult to do and results in serious adversity but, because of its importance, we do it anyway.

Jonah tried to run away from his life-work. And, his story points out the importance of finding and doing your life- work. You will face difficulty when doing your life-work, but, the difficulty, disquiet and distress you experience when not doing it, may be greater. I learn from the story of Jonah, never run away from work. **Never seek to avoid challenging work, especially work designed to enhance the well-being of others.** One of the great secrets to life is, **to get to do the things you want to do, you have**

to learn to do the things you don't want to do.

In nature there is no opinion about work purpose assignments. This is the main reason for nature's magnificent success. All of nature works. All of nature works at what it was made to work at. Nature does its work. Nature has no hesitation. It asks no questions. It engages in no debate. It expresses no different opinions. It just works. It does what it was made to do, it works.

I Kings 17:1-16 says: (NIV-Life Application)

> *Now Elijah the Tishbite, from Tishbe in Gilead, said to Ahab, "As the Lord, the God of Israel, lives, whom I serve, there will be neither dew nor rain in the next few years except at my word."*
> *²Then the word of the Lord came to Elijah:*
> *³"Leave here, turn eastward and hide in the Kerith Ravine, east of the Jordan. ⁴You will drink from the brook, and I have ordered the ravens to feed you there."*
>
> *⁵So he did what the Lord had told him. He went to the Kerith Ravine, east of the Jordan, and stayed there. ⁶The ravens brought him bread and meat in the morning and bread and meat in the evening, and he drank from the brook. ⁷Some time later the brook dried up because there had been no rain in the land.*

⁸*Then the word of the Lord came to him:* ⁹*'Go at once to Zarephath of Sidon and stay there. I have commanded a widow in the place to supply you with food.'* ¹⁰*So he went to Zarephath. When he came to the town gate, a widow was there gathering sticks. He called to her and asked, "would you bring me a little water in a jar so I may have a drink?"* ¹¹*As she was going to get it, he called, "And bring me, please, a piece of bread."*

¹²*"As surely as the Lord your God lives,"* *she replied, "I don't have any bread-only a handful of flour in a jar and a little oil in a jug. I am gathering a few sticks to take home and make a meal for myself and my son, that we may eat it-and die."*

¹³*Elijah said to her, "Don't be afraid. Go home and do as you have said. But first make a small cake of bread for me from what you have to bring me, and then make something for yourself and your son."* ¹⁴*For this is what the Lord, the God of Israel says: "The jar of flour will not be used up and the jug of oil will not run dry until the Lord gives rain on the land."*

¹⁵ *She went away and did as Elijah told her. So there was food every day for Elijah and for the woman and her family.* ¹⁶*For the jar of flour was not used up and the jug of oil*

did not run dry, in keeping with the word of the Lord spoken by Elijah.

Notice here that God gave work instructions to the ravens, a part of nature, and to the widow. There was no opinion expressed by the ravens about how difficult it is to feed themselves let alone help feed somebody else. Nature just follows the work purpose assignment built into it. There is no hesitation. There is no doubt. There is no uncertainty. There is no worry. There is just enthusiastic, effective, and efficient work.

However, the widow had serious hesitation. She expressed a strong opinion of concern. She felt and expressed fear. She felt and expressed uncertainty. She felt and expressed doubt. The widow had to be encouraged to do the work necessary to support and sustain life. Her fear had to be removed. Her doubt had to be dispelled. Her uncertainty had to be cleared, and then, she was able to do the work necessary to support and sustain life.

When you resist doing the work necessary to support and sustain life, not only do others suffer, but you suffer as well. The widow in the above account was already in distress, fear, worry, depression, and sadness. The conditions of the drought had caused her to feel her life and her son's life coming to an end. In fact, she was already preparing for death. In her mind she had already given up. She was already in the midst of losing life. She had already concluded that she and her son were going to die. And then when instructions on how to support and sustain life came, she resisted them by insisting and focusing on how bad her circumstances were.

The work of life is simple but not easy. What the widow was asked to do was simple but not easy. The work of life is unconditional. The work of life does not depend on whether or not it's a sunshiny day. The work of life does not depend on whether or not you are wealthy or poor. It does not depend on how you may or may not feel. It does not depend on how good or bad things look. It does not depend on what you think about whether or not it should be done.

The work of life just must be done, and when it is done, it always brings life supporting and sustaining results for both the doer and the recipient. When the widow decided to do the work she was being asked to do, she decided to live rather than die. **When you make a decision to live, you make a decision to do the work necessary to live. Living is in the work. Living is in the effort.** Living is in the systematic application of energy.

The state of death requires no effort. It requires no energy application. The state of laziness requires little to no effort and energy expenditure. **Death and laziness are always easier than life. Life is work.** It's not surprising therefore, that many choose the easier route, laziness, inactivity, no effort, no energy expenditure, even death. **Choose life, work!**

Life is a choice. Work is a choice. Through Moses, God spoke to His people of yesterday and today in Deuteronomy 30:15-16: *"I have set before you this day life and good, and death and evil... [16]I command you this day to love God, walk in His ways, keep His commandments, statutes and judgments so that you may live and multiply; and God shall bless you in the land that you are going to possess."* Verses 17-18 outline the peril experienced when we choose not to follow God's plan and work assignment. Then, in verse 19-20 God says *"I call heaven and earth to record this day against you, that I have set before you life and death, blessing and cursing. Therefore choose life, that both you and your seed may live;-* [20]*that you may love God, that you may obey God's voice and that you may hold tight to God; for God is life..."*

These words of scripture bring out the point I've been trying to make. Life is work. Life requires work. Life is a choice. Work is a choice. The work God calls for His people to do is the work that makes us strong spiritual beings. Being made "after the image in the likeness of God" we are spiritual beings. The more spiritual work we do, the better and stronger spiritual beings we become. The more spiritually strong we are, the more life we can and do live.

Choosing life is a major cause of life. When you choose life, you are choosing to do the work that results in a better life and more life. For example, when a person who is obese chooses life they are choosing to do the work of exercise and diet management to achieve a better life and subsequently, more life. When a person who is lazy chooses life, they are choosing to do the work of eliminating procrastination and strengthening self-discipline. When a student who is failing chooses life, he/she chooses to do the work of class attendance, homework assignments, class participation, and consistent studying. When a husband or wife, in a failing relationship, chooses life, they choose to do the work of focusing on God, love, mutual submission and mutual support.

Fulfilling work is a win-win situation. **Work designed to enhance the well-being of others is always fulfilling.** It is win-win because the targeted "others" experienced the joy that results from receiving needed help or assistance, and you experience the nourishment and nurturing of fulfillment. Jesus said on one occasion to his disciples, *"My nourishment comes from doing the will of him that sent me, and finishing his work."* John 4:34. My interpretation of this scripture is that p*urposeful, 'other' centered work is nourishing.*

The work Jesus was sent to do was entirely "other" centered. It was extremely difficult and challenging. It was of the highest importance and value. It significantly added to the life of others and it brought Him joy.

Everything God made was made to do work. Work is life. Life is work. To live you have to work at it. Worthwhile work is living. Worthwhile work is worth living for. Worthwhile work is why we live. Worthwhile work is work that contributes to life. Worthwhile work is virtually always directed outside of yourself.

In the first work assignment given in the Bible in Genesis 2:15, Adam was instructed to *"dress and keep the garden."* After Adam was given his work assignment, then he was given instructions on what he could eat and how he should behave to best care for and look after himself. Everything on earth has a work assignment. This work assignment is its purpose.

The preposition "to" has as one of its meanings, " for the purpose of." This is its meaning in the verse, Genesis 2:15, where it says, *"And the Lord God took the man and put him in the Garden of Eden to dress it and keep it."* In other words, Adam was placed in the Garden of Eden "for the purpose of " dressing and keeping the Garden of Eden. The first life instructions Adam received were about work. The first instruction given to the first man was to work.

We are here to do work. All of creation is here to do work. To exist we must work. To exist all creation must do work. Everything God made was made to do work. **Any life that does not do the work of life will not remain alive. Life has to do the work of life to keep the life going that supports life.** Everything God made has a work assignment/purpose from its inception. Nothing made by God was made just for the fun of it. All of creation has a purpose/work assignment, and life depends on that purpose/work assignment being carried out.

For example, in the human body, the heart is a muscled chamber designed for the work purpose of pumping blood to and throughout the whole body. Every part of the body must receive blood or it dies. So, the heart must do its work assignment to provide life-sustaining blood to every part of the body. The work of the heart is to support and enhance life. If and when the heart malfunctions and does not effectively and efficiently perform its pumping function, the life of the body is compromised, and, if the life of the body is compromised, so too is the life of the heart. The heart does its work like there is a built-in knowledge that its very life depends on it. The same is true for every other organ and system of the body. The same is true for every organism in nature.

Work, in a real sense, is a gift. It is a gift that affords opportunity. It is a gift available to all equally. It is a gift that gives and keeps on giving. It is a gift that grows the giver and the recipient. It is a gift from God. Everything made by God was made to do work. This is saying that everything made by God was given the gift of work or the ability to do work. Viewed as a gift, work takes on new meaning.

Gifts from God represent power or ability to achieve purpose. All of God's power has a process by means of which it is realized or achieved. Inherent in the power is the process. **God is as much about process as power.** With God they are one and the same. The power is the process. So then, **work is a gift that represents the power and process to**

support and sustain life. Work also is a gift that grows and enhances life. Work adds to life. **The ability to grow and enhance life is a gift called work.**

Everything God made was given that gift. In the human condition, *what you do much and well, you do better and best.* **It is in the "doing" that the much, well, better and best is achieved.**

> Matthew 25:14-30: (NIV-Life Application) *"Again, it (the kingdom of heaven) will be like a man going on a journey, who called his servants and entrusted his property to them. ¹⁵To one he gave five talents of money, to another two talents, and to another one talent, each according to his ability. Then he went on his journey. ¹⁶The man who had received the five talents went at once and put his money to work and gained five more. ¹⁷So also, the one with two talents gained two more. ¹⁸But the man who had received the one talent went off, dug a hole in the ground and hid his master's money. ¹⁹After a long time the master of those servants returned and settled accounts with them.*
>
> *²⁰The man who had received five talents brought an additional five. 'Master,' he said, 'you entrusted me with five talents. See, I have gained five more.' ²¹His master replied, 'Well done thy, good and faithful servant! You have been faithful with a few things; I will put you in charge of many*

things. Come and share your masters' happiness!' ²²The man with two talents also came. 'Master,' he said, 'you entrusted me with two talents; see, I have gained two more.' ²³His master replied 'Well done, good and faithful servant! You have been faithful with a few things; I will put you in charge of many things. Come and share your master's happiness!'

²⁴Then the man who had received the one talent came. 'Master,' he said, 'I knew that you are a hard man, harvesting where you have not sown and gathering where you have not scattered seed. ²⁵So I was afraid and went out and hid your talent in the ground. See, here is what belongs to you.' ²⁶His master replied, 'You wicked, lazy servant! So you knew that I harvest where I have not sown and gather where I have not scattered seed? ²⁷Well then, you should have put my money on deposit with the bankers, so that when I returned I would have received it back with interest. ²⁸Take the talent from him and give it to the one who has ten talents.

²⁹For everyone who has will be given more, and he will have an abundance. Whoever does not have, even what he has will be taken from him. ³⁰And throw that worthless servant outside, into the darkness, where there will be weeping and gnashing of teeth.'"

A main point of this parable is work. The main point of this parable is faith. Faith and work are two sides of the same coin. **Work is faith. Faith is work. Work is life. We live by faith.** We walk by faith. Faith is the driving force behind work. Faithful people are hardworking people. Faithful people work. **A person's faith is evidenced by their work. A person's work is evidence of their faith.**

Notice that this parable points out that life's rewards result from work. **You don't get something for nothing. In fact, you don't even get to keep what you've been given, without work. Life, and the blessings of life, require work.** They require expenditure of energy.

Matthew 25:21 says, *"Well done thy good and faithful servant, you have been faithful over a few things, I will make you ruler over many. Enter into the joy of your Lord."* This verse is the essence of this parable. It captures and capsulizes everything Jesus was trying to get across about the kingdom of God. When you work at life faithfully, consistently and persistently with a focus on being of service to others, you will succeed and experience the life enhancing joy that results from successful accomplishment.

Let's look again at the human body. The muscular skeletal system is designed to support the body's structure and provide locomotion. Essentially the muscular skeletal system is the principal system responsible for the body's movement, sitting, standing, running, walking, lifting, handling, pushing, pulling, talking, touching, and holding. Exercise that is consistent and persistent strengthens the muscular skeletal system. Exercise builds strength. Exercise is work. It is the systematic expenditure of energy. The more consistent and persistent you are with exercise, the stronger your muscular skeletal system will be. We can add to the life of our muscular skeletal system by doing the work of exercise. This means, we can add to physical life by doing the work of exercise. Exercise enhances muscle. Exercise enhances strength. Exercise enhances life.

This same point is true on the spiritual side. When spiritual muscle is exercised, it too is grown, strengthened and enlivened. The building of physical muscle revolves around endurance, flexibility, resistance. Aerobic (consistent movement) exercise builds endurance. Stretching builds flexibility. Weight lifting builds resistance. The key to achieving results in each area is consistence and persistence. **Work builds capacity.** Capacity is ability. It is potential. Capacity is aptitude, altitude and attitude. It is what you are capable of. **Work enhances what you are capable of.**

Everything God made was made to do work. Work is a wonderful thing. Work is at the foundation of creativity. It is the life force of creativity. Work is joy. Work strengthens. Work empowers. Work builds capacity. Work adds life and adds to life. People with a mind to work go places. They do things. They build. They make progress. They prosper. Nehemiah 4:6. *"So we rebuilt the wall till all of it reached half its height, for the people worked with all their heart."*

To build spiritual capacity you must work. You must do spiritual work. You must do work that enhances your spiritual endurance, expands your spiritual reach and increases your spiritual strength and/ or resistance. Self- discipline, service, faith and patience are four work pillars on which building spiritual capacity stands.

Self-discipline is the strength to say no when you should say no and stick to it; and the strength to say yes when you should say yes and carry through on it. Service is the essence of spiritual work. The more of it you do, the more blessed you become. Faith is the desire, drive and determination to achieve a positive end result. Faith keeps you going through tough times, against all odds and adversity. **Patience is persistence that appreciates the journey but never loses sight of the destination.**

The work of self-discipline, service, faith and patience builds spiritual capacity. It's worth repeating that work is a gift. It is the means by which people can do more and better. It is a gift given to all equally. **The gift of work says, all have the opportunity and ability to do more and better. Work is a life gift. It is**

a gift for life. It is a gift that adds life and adds to life.

In the area of health it is known that to do better you must know better. Certainly this is true in all other areas of life activity as well. To do better you must know better. However, just because you know better does not mean you will do better. There must be a catalyst, something to trigger the "doing" and there must be the strength or capacity to do it. Just because hydrogen and oxygen occupy the same space does not mean water (H20) will be produced. Hydrogen and oxygen must come together in the right proportions and in the right environment to produce water.

Likewise just because an individual has a need and knowledge of how to address that need does not mean the need will be addressed. Just because an obese person is aware of their need to lose weight and knows how to lose it, does not mean they will. Just because a person in serious financial trouble is aware of and knows their need to stop spending money they don't have, and knows how to stop, does not mean they will stop spending. There must be a catalyst, and, there must be the strength to sustain it.

Awareness of a problem and knowledge of how to solve it does not address the problem. **Doing the work of the solution solves the problem. Work is necessary to address life challenges.** Awareness and knowledge are only the necessary prelude to the work that must be done to achieve desired results. People too often learn what needs to be done, but don't do it, and it's not because they don't want to do it. They want to do it. They want to lose weight. They want to get out of debt. They want to finish their degree. They want to get good grades. They want to exercise regularly, but they are unwilling to do the work necessary to make it happen. *They don't want to do the work needed to bring the solution into existence.*

Work can be difficult but it's always rewarding. Worthwhile work is especially rewarding. But even mundane, routine work is beneficial. It is interesting, even fascinating to note that essentially all of the individual parts of nature seem to have as their primary work responsibility, something mundane and/or very routine. Rivers flow. Mountains stand. Grass and flowers grow. Mountains stand. Butterflies pollinate. Honeybees pollinate. Earth rotates. Temperatures rise. Temperatures fall. Fish swim. Birds fly. Birds help balance the ecology. Trees bud, blossom, grow leaves, bear fruit, shed fruit, shed leaves.

Then after winter, they repeat the process. They bud, blossom, grow leaves, bear fruit, shed fruit and shed leaves. Over and over again, year in and out, trees do the same thing. There is no variance, no divergence. The trees, the birds, the bees, the sun, the soil, the rivers, the oceans, the fish, the mountains all do the same thing over and over again. They have a routine. They follow their routine. They work their routine exactly…There is no sense of boredom or frustration. There is no evidence that the various elements of nature get weary or tired of doing what they do. Each part of nature seems to do its work at its highest and best each time it does it. And herein lies much of the magnificence, majesty and beauty of nature.

Each time a part does the work it was designed to do, it does it like it's the first time. It does it at its highest and best. Despite the apparent routineness, mundaneness, plain paths and simple procedures that are repeated over and over again, there is always a freshness and pureness with which the routines, paths and procedures are followed. Pureness, freshness, innocence, honesty and sincerity are always attractive. These qualities characterize the elements of nature and how they work. These characteristics represent one half of why nature is so magnificent and such a wonderful manifestation of the awesomeness of God.

The other half of the magnificence of nature is in its effectiveness. It gets results. Nature does the work it is supposed to do. Nature does its work without fail. Nature is consistent. It is persistent, it works. It gets results. There is nothing more valuable or more beautiful than something that does what it is designed to do, the way it was designed to do it, when it is designed to do it.

In human beings this would be called righteousness. That is, doing the right thing, in the right way, for the right reason at the right time. In humans, righteousness is the pureness, freshness, innocence, honesty and sincerity we see in nature. Whenever and wherever humans experience righteousness, it is always magnetically attractive. Just as in nature, in the human condition, righteousness is a magnificent and wonderful manifestation of the awesomeness of God.

What are the Leading Causes of LIFE?

Righteousness is work. Righteousness is the work God designed humans to do. We know this because He is always the same "yesterday, today and forever." God never acts out of character. If righteousness (pureness, freshness, innocence, honesty and sincerity) is built by God into one part of creation, it is built into all parts of creation.

Humans were designed for righteousness. Humans were designed to do the work of righteousness. Righteousness is godliness. **Humans are wired for godliness because humans are wired by God.**

So, if godly qualities are built into nature, godly qualities are built into humans. If nature was designed to reflect the characteristics of God, certainly humans were. If nature was designed to do work, humans were designed to do work. If nature was designed to work at its highest and best, humans were designed to work at its highest and best. If nature was designed to be effective and get results, certainly human were also. If nature was designed to be pure, fresh, innocent, honest and sincere, humans were designed to be pure, fresh, innocent, honest and sincere. Nature does the work it was designed to do. It has no other option.

Humans have the gift/ability of options. Humans have the gift ability of thinking. We have the gift ability of choice. And unfortunately, often humans think and choose options that are not righteous. In other words, humans often choose options that are outside of what they were designed to choose. By definition, this means, not achieving full potential.

Life that adds to life is the work of nature. Life that adds to life is the way nature works. Life that adds to life is who Jesus is. Life that adds to life is who God is. Life that adds to life is what righteousness is. Life that adds to life is who humans are designed to be. True work is life. Work builds capacity. Capacity is life. So, true work is life that adds to life. Work is a gift that keeps giving. The more it's utilized, the more it gives. Work is a gift that gives to the giver and give-ee. The more you give work, the more work gives to you. A Biblical example of this point is Noah, who is described as a "righteous man."

Genesis 6:8-22 (NIV-Life Application):

[8]...But Noah found favor in the eyes of the Lord.

[9]This is the account of Noah. Noah was a righteous man blameless among the people of his time, and he walked with God, [10]Noah had three sons: Shem, Ham and Japheth.
[11]Now the earth was corrupt in God's sight and was full of violence. [12]God saw how corrupt the earth had become, for all the people on earth had corrupted their ways.
[13]So God said to Noah, "I am going to put an end to all people, for the earth is fill with violence because of them. I am surely going to destroy both them and the earth. [14] So make yourself an ark of cypress wood; make rooms in it and coat it with pitch inside and

out. ⁱ⁵ This is how you are to build it: The ark is to be 450 feet long, 75 feet wide and 45 feet high. ¹⁶Make a roof for it and finish the ark to within 18 inches of the top. Put a door in the side of the ark and make lower, middle and upper decks. ¹⁷I am going to bring floodwaters on the earth to destroy all life under the heavens, every creature that has the breath of life in it. Everything on earth will perish. ¹⁸But I will establish my covenant with you, and you will enter the ark—you and your sons and your wife and your sons' wives with you. ¹⁹You are to bring into the ark two of all living creatures, male and female, to keep them alive with you. ²⁰Two of every kind of bird, of every kind of animal and of every kind of creature that moves along the ground will come to you to be kept alive. ²¹You are to take every kind of food that is to be eaten and store it away as food for you and for them."

²²Noah did everything just as God commanded him.

This passage of scripture details God commanding Noah to build an ark. It outlines specific details on how the ark was to be built. The righteous God speaks to a righteous man and gives righteous commands, which he follows righteously. In other words The righteous person does righteous work. The righteous person works righteously. The righteous person does the right thing in the right way for the right reason at the right time. The work gets done. The work is done right. The work is done in a way that contributes to or adds to life. Because the work on the ark was done in the way God commanded, the ark worked as it was designed to.

All work designed by God works perfectly. Work that follows God's design works just like it is supposed to. Work that follows God's design is always designed to add to life. Work that follows God's design will protect life, produce life, promote life and prosper life. The following passage about Noah makes this point further.

> Genesis 7:14-23 (NIV-Life Application):
> *[14]They had with them every wild animal according to its kind, all livestock according to their kinds, every creature that moves along the ground according to its kind and every bird according to its kind, everything with wings. [15]Pairs of all creatures that have the breath of life in them came to Noah and entered the ark. [16]The animals going in were male and female of every living thing, as God had commanded Noah. Then the Lord shut him in.*
> *[17]For forty days the flood kept coming on the earth, and as the waters increased they lifted the ark high above the earth. [18]The waters rose and increased greatly on the earth, and the ark floated on the surface of the water. [19]They rose greatly on the earth, and all the*

high mountains under the entire heavens were covered. [20] *The waters rose and covered the mountains to a depth of more than twenty feet.* [21]*Every living thing that moved on the earth perished—birds, livestock, wild animals, all the creatures that swarm over the earth, and all mankind.* [22]*Everything on dry land that had the breath of life in its nostrils died.* [23]*Every living thing on the face of the earth was wiped out; men and animals and the creatures that move along the ground and the birds of the air were wiped from the earth. Only Noah was left, and those with him in the ark.* [24]*The waters flooded the earth for a hundred and fifty days.*

Follow God's design. Be righteous. Do righteous work. Work righteously. Righteous work, done righteously, protects life, produces life, promotes life and prospers life. **Be righteous. Do the work of righteousness. Work righteously.**

Remember, righteousness is never conditional. It does not depend on the circumstances. Righteousness is or it is not. Whenever it is, it's always successful. In another biblical account, the importance of working righteously is made. Jacob was deceived, manipulated, used and misused by the selfishness of his uncle Laban. Laban deccived Jacob into working 14 years for the hand of Rachel whom he loved. The normal time was 7 years. However, after the first years, Laban declared that Jacob had to first marry Leah his eldest daughter. Then, it would require an additional seven years to receive Rachel in marriage. Additionally, Laban cheated Jacob by changing his wages ten times (Gen 31: 6-7). Yet Jacob worked righteously. And he got results.

Genesis 31: 36-42 (NIV-Life Application):

[36]Jacob was angry and took Laban to task. "What is my crime" he asked Laban. "What sin have I committed that you hunt me down? [37]Now that you have searched through all my goods, what have you found that belongs to your household? Put it here in front of your relatives and mine, and let them judge between the two of us. [38]I have been with you for twenty years now. Your sheep and goats have not miscarried, nor have I eaten rams from your flocks. [39]I did not bring you animals torn by wild beasts; I bore the loss myself. And you demanded payment from me for whatever was stolen by day or night. [40]This was my situation: The heat consumed me in the daytime and the cold at night, and sleep fled from my eyes. [41]It was like this for the twenty years I was in your household. I worked for you fourteen years for your two daughters and six years for your flocks, and you changed my wage ten times. If the God of my father, the God

of Abraham and the fear of Isaac, had not been with me, you would surely have sent me away empty-handed. But God has seen my hardship and the toil of my hands, and last night he rebuked you."

Working righteously builds physical capacity. Working righteously builds spiritual capacity. Working righteously builds a positive reputation. Working righteously builds other peoples' interest in and demand for you and your expertise. Working righteously adds life and adds to life. **Be righteous. Work righteously.**

A wonderful expression of the beneficial results of working righteously is the story of Jason McElwain. Jason is a 17-year-old autistic child who did not speak his first words until after his fifth birthday. Autism is a brain disorder that retards one's ability to communicate, form relationships and respond appropriately to one's surroundings. Jason loves basketball but with his 5'9" and 130-pound frame added to his autism, he just did not have the talent ability to make his Greece-Athena High School team in upstate New York. But, he loved the game so much he became team manager just to be around the game. He took his work seriously.

First, he was manager of the junior varsity, then, the varsity. He practiced with the team all year long and then, at game time, he faithfully put on his dress shirt and tie and cheered the team on from the bench. According to "The Leaven.com" the official newspaper of The Archdiocese of

Kansas City in Kansas, the coach commented, "When you see a kid that dedicated, you want to see him rewarded."

The coach asked Jason to put on a uniform for the last game of the season for the possibility - - not guarantee - - of playing. In the last four minutes of the last quarter of the last game of the season, with a sizable lead, the coach called the name of Jason to enter the game. The fans cheered. The coach prayed he would get at least one basket. His mother cried for the opportunity her son was being given, knowing how much it meant to him. He missed his first two shots terribly. And then he started making 3-point shots one after another. He made six of them and a two pointer ending up with 20 points in the last four minutes of the last quarter of the last game of the season. He was the highest scorer of the game. The crowd was in a frenzy. They cheered wildly and along with his teammates, carried Jason off the court.

A fellow student captured Jason's performance on a video camera. It was shown on local television stations. Then, it was picked up by ESPN, CNN and Good Morning America. He appeared on the Oprah Winfrey Show and met with President Bush. And to put the icing on the cake, Magic Johnson, former professional basketball superstar, called Jason with an offer to produce a movie about his life.

In four minutes of basketball play, Jason McElwain's life was transformed from that of a team manager to a national celebrity signing autographs. But, I maintain, Jason's stardom was not achieved in the four minutes. The four minutes represents the opportunity of which he took advantage. **His stardom was achieved in the work he did day in and day out practicing with the team and managing the team.** His faithful, dedicated, consistent work created an environment that gave him the opportunity where he blossomed. He was faithful over his assignment as team manager and in his practicing with the team. His faithful work gave him the opportunity and the capacity to shine.

"Everything God made was made to do work." Those who take this seriously and adhere to it closely will experience more, new, wider and deeper life. **Work, especially faithful, righteous work is a cause of life.**

Chapter 5
Everything God Made Was Made To Work At Its Highest And Best Through Relationship With Everything Else God Made

God is all about relationship. Relationship makes life work. Relationship makes the universe work. Relationship is how nature works. Relationship is how humans achieve their highest and best.

The relationships in nature are the best reflections and metaphors for the importance God places on connections, networking, relationships. For example, the planets of our solar system are in an orbital relationship with the sun. There is a gravitational connection and attraction that holds the planets in their places, and earth, to support life, must be held precisely at 93,000,000 miles away. Closer would burn us up, and farther away would freeze us up. The sun supports life here on earth. If the sun goes dark, so would life on earth. Vegetation requires the sun to do what it does. Humans require the sun and vegetation to do what they do. Vegetation requires the harmonious stewardship of humans for it to flourish. To do what it does, vegetation uses the carbon dioxide humans exhale. To do what we do, humans use the oxygen that vegetation puts off. So, in a wonderful balance of give and take, humans take in what vegetation does not need which is what it gives off; and vegetation takes in what humans don't need which is what we give off. Give and take benefits are the foundation of a good, healthy synergistic relationship. **Real relationship is synergistic - everybody benefits.**

One of the best examples of synergistic relationship is the human body. Depending on how you break them down or divide them up, there are nine or ten systems in the human body: Nervous, cardio-vascular, respiratory, urological, muscular-skeletal, endocrine, gastro-intestinal, reproductive and immunological. Each of these systems has specialized structures and functions. The muscular-skeletal system is comprised of 206 bones and approximately 634 muscles. This means, there are about 840 parts working together to form the muscular-skeletal system. Each of these parts has an individual role. But, none of the individual parts, no matter how well it functions, can cause the human body to move from one place to another. All 840 parts, working together, is what makes the body move.

Relationship is simply, connection. But, more than that, relationship is synergistic connection. **Relationship is connection that is mutually beneficial, mutually helpful, mutually stimulating, mutually giving.**

The 840 parts referred to above is not the entire muscular-skeletal system. There are tendons, muscles and bones attached together and to each other. Each part has a part. Each part plays its part. Each part does its part at its highest and best. The normal functioning of the system depends on this point. **The foundation of any system is each part doing its part, at its highest and best.**

Healthy relationship maximizes the performance of each part. Healthy relationship is mutually enlivening. Healthy relationship enhances life. Healthy relationship adds life and adds to life. **Healthy relationship is a major cause of life.**

Let's look again at the human body. Each of the systems of the body has its singular, unique and extremely important function. Each system plays a very important role. In fact, without the role of each system the body will either be severely compromised, weakened, disabled, or, it will die.

The gastrointestinal system, responsible for the intake and processing of food and water, has a role necessary for the life of the entire body. Without the gastrointestinal system and what it does, the body will be severely compromised and eventually die.

The respiratory system is responsible for the intake of oxygen and the elimination of carbon dioxide. The process of breathing is essential to life. Without what the lungs do, the body will die in minutes. The lungs play a unique role in the body that contributes to the life of the body.

It is the same with **the cardiovascular system**. This system is comprised of a pump (the heart) connected to thousands of miles of piping (blood vessels) which together transport oxygen, nutrients and hormones to all parts of the body in the blood and it picks up and brings back items for elimination. The cardiovascular system is the body's transportation system. It delivers and picks up. One part (the ventricles and arteries) is for delivery of necessary life giving substances. The other part (atria and the veins) is for returning to the heart blood that needs purging and replenishing. The cardiovascular system plays a unique and important role in the body. Without it, the body cannot live.

The pattern is the same for the remaining systems as well. All of the systems play unique and important roles in the human body. Without each of them, the body would be severely compromised and eventually die.

Consider the body without **the urological system**. This system's function is to eliminate and thereby prevent the accumulation of life damaging waste.

How about **the all-important nervous system**. Essentially everything we do, consciously and unconsciously is mediated through the nervous system. No system is more unique or more necessary to life than the nervous system and certainly, without the nervous system, the body cannot live.

As unique, fascinating and awesome as all of these systems are, they are able to do what they do only through relationship. Outside of a connection to each other, each of the systems would be nothing but a pile of dead tissue. The uniqueness, awesomeness, productivity, consistence and persistence of each system all mean nothing outside of their connection to each other.

Relationship is key. It is the relationship of these systems (their connection to each other) that makes possible what they do individually and, what happens as a result of what they do individually. In other words, it is their connectedness—their relationship that causes their individual life and as a consequence, life for the whole body.

Life at its highest and best emerges through relationship. Life is generated, supported, enhanced and maximized through relationship. The highest things in life come through relationship. The best things in life come through relationship. Most things in life come through relationship.

All of nature works through relationship. It's all connected. Every part of nature has a part to play to insure its overall successful functioning. Nature is tied together (connected) in a mutually beneficial, mutually helpful, mutually stimulating and mutually giving relationship.

Ecology is the branch of biology that deals with the relationship between living organisms and their environment. In nature there is an ecological balance that is established and maintained through the relationships of all the component parts. Without this ecological balance there can be no life.

The interesting thing about ecological balance is that it represents an interaction between the animal kingdom, large and small, the insect kingdom, small and smaller, the plant kingdom, large and small, the atmospheric elements (sun, wind, soil and water) and invisible microscopic organisms like bacteria and viruses. The biodiversity of nature is all tied together by an incredible ecological balance. This ecological balance represents life at its highest and best. Literally, there are millions and millions of parts doing their part and out of this environment, emerges life.

According to Dr. Edward Wilson in his book, *The Diversity of Life,* tropical rain forests, though occupying only 6 percent of the earth's land surface, are believed to contain more than half of the species or organisms on earth. This of course means in addition to the teamwork relationship that exists to create the general life supporting ecological balance of nature, there is something specific going on in tropical areas that produces even more life. This extra something is not just one thing. The things responsible for more life in the tropics than elsewhere include: more solar (the sun) energy; more stability in the climate (i.e. there is little temperature and other atmospheric change from season to season and year to year); more area affected by more sun and stability. And so, more life seems to result from more area affected by more and more consistent sun and moisture. **The bottom line in all of this is, relationship is at the foundation and peak of life.**

Nowhere in nature does one get the picture of life being something that is, or emerges out of a single, stand alone, unattached, unconnected, unaffected entity. Life, especially life in abundance, is a result of a related number of things performing a related number of functions, all directed toward and designed to achieve one purpose.

The contribution of relationship to abundant life is manifested at every level of nature, large and small, macrocosmically and microcosmically. Another example from Dr. Wilson's book refers to soil. The very soils of the world are created by organisms. Plant roots shatter rocks to form much of the grit and pebbles of the basic substrate. But soils are much more than fragmented rock. They are complex ecosystems with vast arrays of plants, tiny animals, fungi and microorganisms assembled in delicate balance, circulating nutrients in the form of solutions and tiny particles. A healthy soil literally breathes and moves. Its microscopic equilibrium sustains natural ecosystems and croplands alike.

What all this says is, even dirt is a set of complementary, synergistic relationships with each part doing its part to make dirt's overall contribution to life. **Life at its highest and best is, and emerges out of a set of complimentary and synergistic relationships.** Life at its highest and best does not, indeed cannot occur in isolation and separation. **In fact life at its highest and best is a magnificent reflection of relationship and, relationship that is complimentary and synergistic is a magnificent reflection of life at its highest and best.**

Everything God made was made to work at its highest and best through relationship with everything else God made. Life contributes to life. The more life you have around you the more life you live. Better, the more life with which you are connected or interconnected, the more life you will live. **Relationships enhance life.** Relationship is necessary to life. Life is a complex multiplicity of connected complimentary and synergistic entities, functions, and events.

This is a God inspired principle. This principle exists and applies throughout nature from top to bottom and from side to side. It exists and applies throughout the Bible. For example, in the very beginning, the Biblical description of creation is one that makes it clear that life is and emerges out of relationship.

Genesis 1:1-27 (NIV-Life Application):
In the beginning God created the heavens and the earth. ²Now the earth was formless and empty, darkness was over the surface of the deep, and the Spirit of God was hovering over the waters.
³And God said, "Let there be light," and there was light. ⁴God saw that the light was good, and he separated the light from the darkness. ⁵God called the light "day" and the darkness he called "night". And there was evening, and there was morning—the first day.
⁶And God said, "Let there be an expanse between the waters to separate water from water." ⁷So God made the expanse and separated the water under the expanse from

the water above it. And it was so. ⁸ God called the expanse "sky." And there was evening, and there was morning – the second day.
⁹And God said, "Let the water under the sky be gathered to one place, and let dry ground appear." And it was so. ¹⁰God called the dry ground "land", and the gathered waters, he called "seas." And God saw that it was good.

¹¹Then God said, "Let the land produce vegetation: seed-bearing plants and trees on the land that bear fruit with seed in it, according to their various kinds." And it was so. ¹²The land produced vegetation: plants bearing seed according to their kinds and trees bearing fruit with seed in it according to their kinds. And God saw that it was good. ¹³And there was evening, and there was morning—the third day.
¹⁴And God said, "Let there be lights in the expanse of the sky to separate the day from the night, and let them serve as signs to mark seasons and days and years,
¹⁵and let them be lights in the expanse of the sky to give light on the earth." And it was so. ¹⁶God made two great lights—the greater light to govern the day and the lesser light to govern the night. He also made the stars. ¹⁷God set them in the expanse of the sky to give light on the earth, ¹⁸to govern the day and the night, and to

separate light from darkness. And God saw that it was good. [19]And there was evening, and there was morning—the fourth day.
[20]And God said, "Let the water teem with living creatures, and let birds fly above the earth across the expanse of the sky." [21]So God created the great creatures of the sea and every living and moving thing with which the water teems, according to their kinds and every winged bird according to its kind. And God saw that it was good. [22]God blessed them and said, "Be fruitful and increase in number and fill the water in the seas, and let the birds increase on the earth." [23]And there was evening, and there was morning—the fifth day.
[24]And God said, "Let the land produce living creatures according to their kinds: livestock, creatures that move along the ground, and wild animals, each according to its kind." And it was so. [25]God made the wild animals according to their kinds: the livestock according to their kinds, and all the creatures that move along the ground according to their kinds. And God saw that it was good.

[26]Then God said, "Let us make man in our image, in our likeness, and let them rule over the fish of the sea and the birds of the air, over the livestock, over all the earth, and over all the creatures that move along the ground." [27]So God created man in his

own image, in the image of God he created him; male and female he created them.

This first chapter of Genesis describes the creation of the environment of man and eventually, man. It is interesting to note that the environment of man came first. God put in place first, the life supporting environment that man would need to survive, live and prosper.

The life importance and significance of relationship is reflected in the creation account. Fish need water. Plants need soil. Animals need the oxygen rich atmosphere. Plants need water. Animals need water. Fish need oxygen. Everything needs the sun. The environment established by God is an environment that functions at its highest and best through relationship. These relationship connections are necessary to support the life of the environment and that of humans. Theology (God) instructs ecology (balanced environment) which supports biology or humanity. The more humanity is aligned with divinity, the more it will be aligned with ecology. People in a healthy relationship with God will shape a healthy relationship with the environment, God's creation. We all should be environmentalists. The environment is supporting us. We should support it.

In Genesis 2:18 God says, *"It is not good for man to be alone. I will make him a helper suitable for him."* Up to this point everything God had done generated the evaluation that "it was good." This is the first time in Genesis that 'not good' is used in reference to anything done by God and I believe it's not by accident that the 'not good' refers to man being alone. This of course points to the importance God places on relationship.

God establishes and blesses 'relationship' from the very outset of human activity. Relationship is established as the foundation of marriage, family, community and society. Relationship is established as the means by which new humans enter in, and are cared for in this world. Relationship is established as the means by which humans achieve their highest and best. In the human condition what is more important than family? What engenders life more than family? What is more important to the foundation of life than family? Indeed it seems quite apparent, even obvious that family is the foundation of life for humans.

Family is the initial passageway through which life comes into existence. Family is the initial structure into which life is placed. Family is the first context provided to shape and guide life. Family is the environment where life starts its beginning growth, development and maturity. **Certainly, family, the initial relationship into which we are all placed, is a leading cause of life.**

What occurs first in Genesis is the establishment of a life supporting environmental context. This includes the establishment of the sun, atmosphere, water and land. Next came plant life, animal life and life in the waters. Then, finally, came humanity. The process, as outlined is reflective of relationship from beginning to end.

First, the ecological context is put in place. That is, a set of connected events that contributes to life are initiated. Then a group of entities with all of their functions are added. And finally, when the life-supporting context is complete, humanity is added. Each big part has a specific role to play.

Humanity's job is to provide fruitful and replenishing supervision and management. I look at this as a process of theologically inspired ecology that supports a biology, which includes humanity whose role is to keep it all going. Theology, ecology, biology, humanity are all in a mutually beneficial, mutually helpful, mutually stimulating, mutually giving relationship.

The life generating principle that characterizes and connects these entities in relationship is giving. **Giving is the essence of a complimentary, synergistic relationship. Relationship is the essence of life at its highest and best.** This means, **giving is the essence of life itself.** Where there is life, there is giving. Where there is giving, there is life. In fact, giving is essential to life. If you want **to live,** give. The more you give, the more you live. The better you give, the better you live.

There is a theory called altruistic egotism. It's meaning is embodied in the definitions of the two words. Altruism means unselfish concern for the welfare of others or selflessness. Egotism is defined as the tendency to consider only one's self and one's own interests or selfishness. So, altruistic egotism then, combines the human need for selflessness with the human tendency towards selfishness. **More simply put, one gives to live.**

All of nature is structured around giving. Each part does its part. There seems to be a built in awareness or consciousness that giving is the route to living. Therefore, each part altruistically does its part with an egoistic mindset that says, this is what I must do to have my life. The principle works. The principle appears to be the philosophy of nature. All life does what it was designed to do because of a built in awareness that in doing so, it achieves life for itself. In other words, the operating philosophy of nature seems to be, **"I get mine when you get yours."**

Applied to the human body, the philosophy works. For example, the gastrointestinal system ingests, breaks down and digests foods. It does this with a singular purpose and focus, to provide life-sustaining nutrition for the body This is what it was made to do. This is its purpose. This is why it's here. Indeed, this is all it knows. This is all it does and it does it perfectly. There seems to be a built in awareness that says, this is my life, to give the process of digestion. Digestion is what I am. Digestion is what I do. Give digestion to others and I will feed and nourish them and in giving to others (the cardiovascular, nervous, respiratory and all other systems) I sustain them and make it possible for them to do what they do, which will sustain me. In other words, I get mine **when** others get theirs.

The lungs must give up the oxygen they have taken, in order to sustain the other organs. Without the oxygen the other organs will shut down and not function. Then, the lungs will no longer receive what they need to remain alive to do their job. The singular purpose and focus of the lungs is to take in oxygen and get rid of carbon dioxide. Its purpose is to take in from the atmosphere what the body needs to carry out a number of reactions necessary to life, and get rid of what will hurt and kill the body if allowed to stay and accumulate. If and when carbon dioxide remains in the body and accumulates, it will eventually cause malfunction, even death. The lungs must do what they do so other organs can receive what they need to live and do what they do.

In this process of giving the function of breathing, the lungs give their contribution to the life of others, thus making it possible for other organs and systems to continue doing what they do that contributes to the life of the lungs. The fulfillment of the purpose of the lungs is tied to the fulfillment of the purpose of the other organs and systems. It's a life cycle. The lungs must do what they do so other organs can do what they do so, the lungs can do what they do.

More than anything else, **relationship is a circle**. It's dynamic, it moves, it rolls and all parts are in positions of importance. All parts are important and play a significant role in the smooth functioning of the circle. When one part malfunctions or discontinues making its contribution, the circle becomes disfigured and no longer moves or rolls as it should, or as it can. **Everything God made was made to work at its**

highest and best through relationship with everything else God made.
There are countless fascinating examples of life- producing, life-sustaining relationships in nature. One exists between plants and the animals that help to spread their seeds. Plants do not and cannot move from place to place as they are planted, but animals do move. So, many fruit bearing plants are in relationship with the many animals that eat their fruit. The relationship unfolds as follows: the plant feeds the animals by producing fruit. The animals eat the fruit. However, the seed of the fruit passes through the digestive tract of the animals and is passed out at another location. Plants help keep animals alive through producing fruit. Animals help keep plants alive by spreading their seeds about.

Even more interesting is additional examples described in Paul Ehrlich's book, *The Machinery of Nature* (Simon & Schuster, 1986), where he describes the following: "...in the course of evolution, some animals have been recruited to help bury seeds as well. One of the neatest tricks in the plant world has been the evolution by some species of special nutritious tissues on their seeds that attract ants. The ants drag the seeds into their nests, eat the special tissues, and leave the rest...seeds of these species that are transported to ant nests are three times as likely to germinate as those that are not, and the young plants growing on the nests are more than four times as likely to live for at least two years." In nature, relationship is key to surviving and thriving. **Life is enhanced through relationship.**

Another example from the same book involves some 900 species of fig plants. Each species of fig plants is pollinated (fertilized) by its own exclusive species of fig wasp. The flowers of the fig plants are tiny and grow outside the fig that people eat. The tiny female wasp enters the fig deposits pollen on the flowers, lays eggs in the flowers, and then dies. The wasp larvae grow inside the flowers, which they consume, and (then) form pupae (the stage just before maturity). The wingless male fig wasps emerge before the females and march around inside the fig looking for flowers containing females. They use their telescoping abdomens to copulate with the females before they emerge from their pupae. The males then die without ever leaving the fig. The winged females emerge, collect pollen from the remaining flowers, and leave that fig in search of another in the proper condition to begin the cycle again.

The concept of relationship, connection, networking, mutual giving and 'altruistic egoism' works across kingdoms. It's not confined just to within kingdoms (e.g. plant to plant; or animal to animal). Abundant life results through mutually beneficial, mutually giving relationships wherever it is found and however it works.

Honeybees avoid freezing in the winter by forming themselves into a round mass (called "balling") and continuously vibrating the muscles of wings to produce heat. Through connection, coming together, working together, relationship--

each giving what they can-- the whole group benefits and lives. The honeybee, which has been noted to have a brain the size of a pinhead, is known to pollinate (fertilize) the plants from which they take nectar. In other words, the honeybee gives back to the plant from which it takes. In doing this, it keeps alive the plants that provide the food that keeps them alive. In fact, the honeybee is responsible for the pollination and production of a large part of agricultural fruit production in America. Estimates are that the honeybee is involved in the production of one-third of our supply, totaling somewhere between 14 and 20 billion dollars annually.

The honeybee, a creature with a brain the size of a pinhead follows a built in success plan that says, you must give to live. It says, I get mine when you get yours. **It says abundant life comes through giving.**

This foundational principle of life exhibited throughout nature, not surprisingly is found in the Bible. **Giving is a keystone of spiritual life as well.** The following scriptures point to the connection between giving and living: (NIV-Life Application)

> *John 3:16 "For God so loved the world that he gave his one and only Son, that whoever believes in him shall not perish but have eternal life."*
>
> *Galatians 6:7 Do not be deceived: God cannot be mocked. A man reaps what he sows.*

2 Corinthians 9:6-7 Remember this: Whoever sows sparingly will also reap sparingly, and whoever sows generously will also reap generously. [7] Each of you should give what you have decided in your heart to give, not reluctantly or under compulsion, for God loves a cheerful giver.

Proverbs 11:24-25 One man gives freely, yet gains even more; another withholds unduly, but comes to poverty." [25] A generous man will prosper; he who refreshes others will himself be refreshed.

Proverbs 19:17 He who is kind to the poor lends to the Lord, and he will reward him for what he has done.

Luke 6:38 "Give, and it will be given to you. A good measure, pressed down, shaken together and running over, will be poured into your lap. For with the measure you use, it will be measured to you."

Matthew 20:25-28 Jesus called them together and said, "You know that the rulers of the Gentiles lord it over them, and their high officials exercise authority over them. [26] Not so with you. Instead, whoever wants to become great among you must be your servant. [27] and whoever wants to be first must be your slave - [28] just as the Son of

Man did not come to be served, but to serve, and to give his life as a ransom for many."

People who give, live. People involved in healthy relationships live more life and live better lives. People live abundant life who live by the principle of, *'I get mine when you get yours.'*

Everything God made was made to work at its highest and best in relationship with everything else God made. Giving is the essence of a complimentary, synergistic relationship. Relationship is at the foundation of abundant life. Giving then, is the essence of life.

In the Bible, no one gave more than Jesus. Jesus lived by the principle of giving. His purpose was to give. His mission was giving. Every place Jesus went He gave. He gave in one way or another. He gave at one level or another but, He was always giving. Jesus said in John 10:10 *"The thief comes to steal, kill and destroy; I am come that they might have abundant life."* **His target for 'abundant life' was "they." The "they" is others.**

Jesus lived a selfless life with the purpose of fostering and adding life to all with whom He made contact. Jesus made a path and left a tail of health, healing, wholeness, cleansing, enabling, resurrection, redirection and restoration. He was always doing for others He was always ministering to others. He was always serving others. **Service is a form of giving. Service is a key to life**. Where there is an atmosphere of service, characterized by highest and best, there is abundant life.

Everybody loves to be served. Everybody loves good service. People will go out of their way to get good service. People remember good service. People are positively impacted by good service. People are changed by good service. People are moved by good service. People are inspired by good service. People are motivated by good service. People are challenged by good service. People are informed by good service. People are enlightened by good service. People are enabled by good service. People are empowered by good service. Isn't abundant life about being changed, moved, inspired, motivated, challenged, informed, enlightened, enabled and empowered? **Good service adds life and adds to life.**

Marriage is probably the most profound human example of how everything God made was made to work at its highest and best through relationship with everything else God made. Of course relationship is the essence of marriage. The word marriage means connection. When things are married they are connected in relationship. When people are married they are connected in relationship. True relationship is connection. True-life connection adds and multiplies the original. True relationship is mutualistic and synergistic, and it is supported and sustained by the giving that makes mutualism and synergism work. Giving is not only implied in but it is the essence of the words mutual and synergy. Successful marriages are characterized by mutuality and synergism. They are characterized by each individual giving to the other. Not just random giving but giving that enhances, enlarges, satisfies and fulfills the other. This point is made by Matthew 7:12 (The Book) *"Do for others what you would like them to do for you. This is the summary of all that is taught in the law and the prophets."*

Relationship or true connection is the foundation for abundant life. **Mutualism is at the foundation of abundant life. Synergism is at the foundation of abundant life. Giving is at the foundation of abundant life.**

Very important in understanding this important life principle is it begins with "Do for others..." This is the essence of what successful marriage and family is all about. It is a "doing for others." The entire Bible is about how to achieve abundant life. Jesus said, at the foundation of abundant life is the principle "Do for others." **Doing for others is driven by loving others. Love is the driving force behind giving. When you love, you give."** In deed, love **is** giving. Giving is sharing. Sharing is caring. Caring is loving. Loving is living. Living is loving and giving. The highest form of love is giving. John 3:16 says it best, *"For God **so loved** the world that **He gave his only son**; that whoever believes in Him should not perish but have, **everlasting** life."* (Author emphasis) I think "eternal life" qualifies as abundant life.

Life in abundance emerges through relationship. Again, marriage is one of if not the most fundamental and profound human example, of what is supposed to be a true-life relationship, a true connection. For a marriage to work, it must be founded on mutualism, each giving to the other. It must be founded on synergism, each giving that that enhances the other. It must be founded on love, the driving force behind each giving to the other.

When you really love, you give. The giving that results from love is highest and best. **The life that results from "highest and best" giving is abundant. Marriages where each give their highest and best to the other flourish.** Relationships characterized by each giving their highest and best to the other, are not only strong, they are alive, fulfilling, filled with joy and extremely productive.

It is not by accident that the Bible frequently uses marriage as a metaphor for an individual's relationship with God. Individuals who are or seek to be Christians are urged, even commanded to 'marry' and be faithful to God and thereby achieve not just abundant life here on earth, but eternal life later.

> Mark 10:28-31 (NIV-Life Application):
> *[28]Peter said to him, "We have left everything to follow you!" [29]"I tell you the truth," Jesus replied, "no one who has left home or brothers or sisters or mother or father or children or fields for me and the gospel [30] will fail to receive a hundred times as much in this present age (homes, brothers, sisters, mothers, children and fields--and with them, persecutions) and in the age to come,*

> *eternal life. ³¹But many who are first will be last, and the last first."*

    This passage emphasizes the priority God places on relationship. It emphasizes what relationship is all about and it emphasizes the consequences or results of relationship. From God's perspective, relationship is about "highest and best." The disciples gave up everything they used to have, know and do. They did this to establish a relationship with Jesus.

    When people are serious about relationship, they give their all. **To be serious about relationship you must give your all.**

    God was serious about relationship with us as He gave His all.
    He gave His son Jesus.
    He gave the very idea of Himself.
    He gave His highest and best.

    Jesus was serious about His relationship with us as He gave His all.
    He gave His power.
    He gave His healing.
    He gave His comfort.
    He gave His support.
    He gave His strength.
    He gave His wisdom.
    He gave His counsel and advice.
    He gave his highest and best.
    He gave His life.

It is clear, the more social relationships you have the more life you will live. Relationship or true connection contributes to health. Health is an essence of life. People involved in mutually synergistic connections (relationships) with other people are healthier than those who are not.

Dr. Bernie S. Siegel in his book, *Love, Medicine & Miracles* (Harper & Rowe, 1988) addresses the health effects of relationship. He states (pgs. 74-75), "New evidence suggests that divorce may be even more devastating to many people, since it's harder to accept that the relationship is really over. Indeed, divorced people have higher rates of cancer, heart disease, pneumonia, high blood pressure and accidental death than married, single or widowed persons. Married men also have one-third the lung cancer incidence of single men." Dr. Siegel's book also notes the following on pg.73: "The level of stress is determined partly by society. Cultures that place the highest value on a combination of individualism and competition are the most stressful. Those that seem to produce the least stress and have the lowest rates of cancer are close-knit communities in which supportive, loving relationships are the norm, and the elderly retain an active role."

Relationship enhances health. Relationship enhances life. Dr. Siegel cites research that shows that, "patients whose rooms had windows that faced an open courtyard, a tree, and the sky got well faster than those whose rooms faced a brick wall" (pg. 49). Relationship with God through nature enhances health and healing and wholeness. Dr.

What are the Leading Causes of LIFE?

Siegel cites a number of what he calls "exceptional patients" whose lives were saved and health enhanced by deciding to live. Their decision virtually always involved loving and giving. They loved themselves. They loved others. They gave to others. They gave to themselves.

The following is one example of many, pgs. 40-41:

> "I have a copy of a letter from a young woman named Louise to a 'rock n' roll doctor,' who had a radio show combining music with medical advice and with whom she became close friends while she was in the hospital.
>
> As a teenager Louise developed cancer of the ovary with metastases to the lungs and abdomen. Her oncologist "gave" her six to twelve months to live with chemotherapy. She told him only God could decide when her number was up, and began to take her life into her own hands.
>
> She left home because of stressful living conditions, got her own apartment, and spent her last ten dollars to place a newspaper ad, looking for other cancer patients who needed her help.
>
> At one point her oncologist had refused her any further treatment because she was "too far gone," but six months after she had taken the path of her own choosing, all her tumors had disappeared. Her doctor couldn't even tell her this out loud. Instead, with tears in

his eyes, he handed her a prescription form on which he'd written, "Your cancer has disappeared." On the day she was supposed to be dead, Louise sent him a joking note asking, "Where should I send the casket?"

The 'rock n' roll doctor' wrote to tell me that, if he hadn't happened to hear me speak about exceptional patients, he probably wouldn't have made the connection between Louise's "miraculous" recovery and her spiritual growth. Instead, it made sense to him, and they both came to one of our ECAP meetings to share the experience.

Louise chose to love and give, making the kind of spiritual and psychological changes that people who experience self-induced healings always make. It takes enormous strength to do this when the voice of authority is telling you you're supposed to die. The problem is, exceptional patients are a minority."

Relationships enhance health. They enhance life. **Everything God made was made to work at its highest and best through relationship with everything else God made**. Humans are enhanced by and through relationship with each other. Humans were made to enhance each other. Humans thrive best when in healthy contact with each other. In *Minding the Body Mending the Mind* Joan Borysenko, MD, 1987 says (pg. 25-26):

"...The effects of stress are buffered by effective coping and also by the love and

What are the Leading Causes of LIFE?

support of other people. Vaillant found that lonely men often became chronically ill by the time they reached their fifties. It's only through our relations with others that we develop the outlook of hardiness and come to believe in our own capabilities and inner goodness. The lonely baby is in no position to become hardy. The lonely adult may have problems sustaining the attitudes of hardiness.

Several years ago, the small town of Roseto, Pennsylvania, raised considerable interest in the scientific community because of its very low rate of death from coronary heart disease. Epidemiologists began to study the Rosetans, expecting to find low levels of the major risk factors for coronary heart disease: cigarette smoking, fat consumption, a sedentary lifestyle, and obesity. They got a big surprise. The Rosetans had terrible health habits. They were high in all the risk factors. It turned out that their protective factor was actually the social fabric of the community. The extended family was alive and well. People tended to stay within Roseto, and so there was a great deal of closeness. People knew one another, their family histories, their joys and sorrows. In Roseto there were plenty of people to listen and to lend a hand when needed. Statistics revealed that when people are moved out of Roseto, their rate of heart attack rose to the predicted level. Social support, the great stress buffer, turned out to be more important than health habits in predicting heart disease."

At a very basic and biological level for example, humans need to touch each other. Humans are better off, more healthy when we touch. Studies have shown that non-romantic, caring touch of one human by another actually has a lowering effect on levels of the stress hormone, cortisol. Further, evidence is clear that newborn babies must be cuddled or touched to thrive. Prematurely born babies have an even greater need to be touched and cuddled.

Everything God made was made to work at its highest and best through relationship with everything else God made. **Nature is diverse.** The essence of diversity is relationship. Nature is diversity in action. Nature is relationship in action. Nature is diversity at its highest and best. Nature is relationship at its highest and best. Nature has one purpose, life. Relationship has one purpose, life. **The diversity of nature has one purpose, life. The diversity of nature is essential to that one purpose.**

The diversity of nature is the route by means of which it achieves its purpose. Life, the purpose of nature, is a function of many contributing parts all in relationship. All parts do their part in relationship to and with all other parts. Nature is successful. In fact, nature is the most successful thing known to human kind. Nature's success is embodied in the fact that life abounds. And nature is responsible for life. Nature, the things made by God, is what keeps life going here on earth. Nature is persistent, consistent, hardworking, resilient. Nature is replenishes.

The element of Nature most responsible for its success is its diversity. **Nature represents the epitome of diversity.** Nature is, literally, millions and billions of parts all working in concert around the song of life. In Nature each part does its part. Each part does its part with what seems to be a built in awareness that says, in order to get, I must first give. The individual parts are designed to sustain the life of the other parts. There is no alternative. There is no option. There is no variance. There is no divergence from its design. What it was made to do, it does. How it was made to do it, is how it does it. Herein is its success. Nature sticks to its built in plan. Nature stays on its own program.

A butterfly was designed to do butterfly things. That's exactly what a butterfly does. That's exactly why there are certain flowers. That's exactly why butterflies have food. That's exactly why there are still butterflies. Honeybees were designed to do honey bee things. That's exactly what honeybees do. That's exactly why honeybees are so successful. Ants were designed to do ant things. That's exactly what they do. That's why they are so successful.

In bee colonies and ant colonies there is division of labor among the members of the colony. For example, in beehives or colonies, there are worker bees, drones, and a queen bee. The worker bees are sterile females. They make the honeycomb, care for the underdeveloped baby bees, care for the queen, clean the hive and gather nectar and pollen. Drones are males. Their job is to breed with the queen. Queen bees lay the eggs that produce the bees that keep the hive alive. Queen bees can lay as many as 1,500 eggs a day, 200,000 eggs in a year.

The workers do what they were designed to do. The drones do what they were designed to do. The queens do what they were designed to do. There is no variance. There is no divergence. There is only success. Drones and workers don't try to be queens. There's no evidence to suggest that they go into an inactive, non-productive, and non-working state of depression because they can't be queens and lay eggs. They do what they do, and their contribution is welcomed and valued. Their contribution sustains and promotes the life of the hive.

Likewise, there is no evidence to suggest that the queens ever seek to do anything but lay eggs. There is no behavior to suggest the queens get hostile towards the workers or drones because she can't be one of them. The queen's contribution is welcomed and valued. Her contribution sustains and promotes the life of the hive. The queen, workers, and drones all seem to work with an in built perfect self-esteem that says, my contribution is welcomed, valued, and consequential. Each seems to have a built in automatic knowledge that says, I do what I do to keep the hive alive.

An inspirational and exciting motto for any group, team, organization, business, family, or relationship is, **keep the hive alive. Keep the**

hive alive! It means all parts **have** a part. It means all parts **play** a part. It means all parts play **their** part. Where all parts do their part, there is success.

A definition of success is, all parts doing their part when, where, and the way they are supposed to do their part. This definition fits the way a healthy body works. All parts do their part when, where, and the way they are supposed to do their part. This definition fits the way a championship team in any sport works. It fits the way any successful business, organization, or institution works. It fits the way any successful family or relationship works.

Hans Selye in his 1974 book, *Stress Without Distress* (published by Signet) describes altruistic egotism:

"Altruistic Egotism was the basis of evolution throughout the ages. The originally simplest forms of life, consisting of individual and totally independent cells, were subject to the relentless law of natural selection; those cells that could not protect themselves soon ceased to exist. It also became apparent, however, that such *pure egocentricity created dangerous antagonisms,* **the advantages of one individual often being acquired to the detriment of others.** Therefore, a certain degree of altruism had to be introduced for egotistic reasons. **Unicellular organisms began to aggregate and form stronger, more complex multi-cellular beings; in** these, certain cells had to give up part of their independence to specialize in nutrition, defense, or locomotion, but thereby the security and survival value of each individual were raised.

I have emphasized-perhaps irritatingly often-that **egotism is an inherent and unavoidable characteristic of life. Yet pure egotism necessarily leads to conflict and insecurity within the community.** Sometimes, brutal sacrifice is indispensable to protect living nature as a whole. In battle, a general must occasionally reach the painful decision of sacrificing a platoon, or even a regiment, to save an army. But the most efficient and pleasant way of combining the advantages of the few with those of the many is the principle of altruistic egotism.

Single cells combined into multi-cellular organisms and these into larger groups on the basis of this principle, although they were not aware of it. Similarly, individual people have formed the co-operative 'mutual insurance' groups of the family, tribes, and nations within which altruistic egotism is the key to success. It is the only way to preserve teamwork, whose value is ever increasing in modern society." (Author emphasis)

The biological foundation of the principle, altruistic egotism, and its operational reality in nature, both serve to authorize its validity as a viable way of life. To the degree that teams, businesses, organizations, institutions, marriages, families, and all other relationships live, breathe, and have their being in this principle, they will succeed. It's guaranteed. Altruistic egotism, as I've already stated, works. It works in all areas of human endeavor.

Think about a business with altruistic egotism as its operational principle. This would be a place where all co-workers would work together based on, "I get mine **when,** you get yours." Workers or staff would be treated by management, supervisors and senior leadership from the perspective, "I get mine **when,** you get yours." Imagine the atmosphere of a workplace where leadership functioned that way!

Consider the effects of customers being told and then being treated by business staff by the principle, "I get mine **when** you get yours." The emphasis on **"when"** means giving comes first. It means serving comes first. It means doing for others comes first.

People are attracted to and support where they are, and feel served. All businesses talk about and understand that customer service is key to a successful business. Customer service is essential to a business. Highest and best customer service causes a business to thrive and prosper. Highest and best customer service is, "doing for others what you want them to do for you." In other words, "I get mine **when** you get yours." Highest and best customer service results when the business operates

A Prescription of Living at Your Highest and Best

like it is biologically tied to the customer and its very life depends on what it does and how it does it, **for** the customer. Highest and best customer service results when a business operates like it is in a life relationship with its customer. Customers will feel this and their behavior will reflect it.

Highest and best customer service is organic. It is based on the organic principle, "I get mine **when** you get yours." That is, it is the life of the business. It is what the business does. It is the way business lives. Highest and best service can only emerge through a true-life connection. It can only emerge through relationship.

A life relationship is a connection that is mutually beneficial, mutually helpful, mutually stimulating, mutually synergistic, and mutually giving. Nature maximizes its existence because there is no dead weight. Nature uses everything. Nature is effective and efficient. Everything in nature is working in concert with everything else in nature. **Everything is working for the same main purpose; life for the whole.** Nature uses all of its components, no matter how big or how small. It puts to use the macroscopic and the microscopic. It uses the oceans and the ants. It uses bees and trees. It uses soil and the sun. It uses manure and bacteria. It uses plants and animals. Nature overlooks nothing. Nature ignores nothing. It discounts nothing. It dismisses nothing. It discards nothing. Nature puts everything to use. Nature maximizes. Nature ties everything in it together in relationship to achieve a common purpose, life.

What are the Leading Causes of LIFE?

The diversity of relationships and the relationships of the diversity are at the core of the abundant life in nature. The diversity of relationships and the relationships of the diversity are at the core of the power, productivity, prolific-ness, persistence, and replenishing of nature.

Likewise, businesses that have a diversity of talents, perspectives, skills, expertise, and experiences all tied together, and serving customers by the operating principle, altruistic egotism, will succeed. Nature is the ultimate model of and for diversity. Nature is the greatest manager of diversity in existence. Nature teaches that where there is an environment that welcomes, values, employs, and empowers, around a common purpose, there will be success.

People succeed where and when what they bring to the table is embraced, esteemed, employed, and empowered. Relationships succeed where and when what individuals bring to them is embraced, esteemed, employed, and empowered. This is what happens in nature. This is why nature is so successfully productive, prolific, persistent, and replenishing. A real strength of nature is not only its diversity and inherent relationships, but, its multiplicity of diverse relationships.

So then, at the core of the strength, power, productivity, prolific-ness, persistence, and replenishing of nature is its multiplicity of diversity. In other words, **diversity is life. Diversity adds life. Diversity promotes life.**

Diversity sustains life. Nature is diverse. Diversity is nature. Diversity is relationships.

Dr. Edward O. Wilson, in his book, *The Diversity of Life* (Harvard University Press, 1992) has this to say about the life enhancing nature of the multiplicity of diversity:

> **"From a few key studies of forests we know that diversity enlarges the capacity of the ecosystem to retain and conserve nutrients. With multiple plant species, the leaf area is more evenly and dependably distributed. Then the greater the number of plant species, the broader the array of specialized leaves and roots, and the more nutrients the vegetation as a whole can seize from every nook and cranny at every hour through all seasons. The extreme reach of biodiversity anywhere may be that attained by the orchids and other epiphytes of tropical forests, which harvest soil particles directly from mist and airborne dust otherwise destined to blow away. In short, an ecosystem kept productive by multiple species is an ecosystem less likely to fail.**
>
> **Field studies show that as biodiversity is reduced,** so is the quality of the service **provided by ecosystems.** Records of stressed ecosystems also demonstrate that the descent can be unpredictably abrupt. As extinction spreads, some of the lost forms prove to be keystone species, whose disappearance brings down other species

and triggers a ripple effect through the demographics of the survivors. The loss of a keystone species is like a drill accidentally striking a power line. It causes lights to go out all over."
(Author emphasis)

One of the most common expressions of relationship and its importance to human interaction, growth, development and accomplishment is, teamwork.

Teamwork is probably most talked about in the arenas of business and sports entertainment. A team is a group of people working or planning together. It is a group of people organized around a common purpose and agenda. It is a group of people in relationship.

Most human activity involves more than one person. Essentially all higher-level human activity involves groups of people (teams) working together (in teamwork) around a common purpose and agenda. The higher the level of activity, the more important teams and teamwork become. The greater the number of people impacted, and the greater the significance of the impact, the greater the importance of teams and teamwork to achieving that impact. The words team and teamwork suggest: (1) identification, (2) specification, (3) specialization, (4) cooperation, (5) integration, (6) connection, (7) interdependence.

A team and teamwork in essence is relationship. Every team, and therefore relationship is characterized by these seven areas;

identification, specificity, specialization, cooperation, integration, connection and interdependence. The best illustration of this is probably a professional sports team.

First of all the **team provides identity**. The team is an identity. The team is named. The team dresses and looks alike. The team has a known way of doing things. People recognize the team through their name, their look and their way of doing things.

Second, the team is a **team for a specific purpose**. It is organized around a common purpose and agenda. A basketball team is organized to play basketball, not football or baseball or soccer or hockey. The very best basketball team would be demolished in a contest with any baseball team or football team.

Third, teams **have specialized roles**. Specialization enhances expertise. It enhances levels of excellence.

Fourth, individuals with specialized role functions **cooperate to operate as a team**. When called for, each part does its part.

Fifth, the cooperating specialized role functions are **integrated into an organized 'whole game plan'**.

Sixth, the organized, integrated game plan **is practiced to the point of a seamless connectedness**. That is, the integrated, cooperating, specialized role functions all become one connected unit called the team.

Seven, the connected, integrated, cooperating specialized **role functions are elevated to the highest level of successful team behavior,**

interdependence. Interdependence is mutual submission to a higher agenda. More than that, it is highest-level performance to support the highest-level performance of others, **all for the purpose of achieving the highest-level agenda.**

I said all this to say, in the human condition, **our highest and best is achieved through relationship.** In team sports, championships are won through teamwork or relationship. **Everything God made was made to work at its highest and best through relationship with everything else God made.**

Chapter 6
Conclusion

At a very early age-- somewhere between 3 and 5 years old-- my father began to say to me, "Boy, when you grow up, you are going to be a doctor." Every time he got a chance, he repeated to me, "Boy, when you grow up, you're going to be a doctor." We didn't even have a lot of college graduates in our family who could serve as role models for me. We were not wealthy by any stretch of the imagination but, my father had a strong belief in God, a strong love for his family and a strong entrepreneurial Spirit. He behaved like he believed he could do whatever he put his mind to; and, he made me believe the same thing.

Over and over in all kinds of settings with all kinds of people he would have me tell people what I was going to be when I grew up. After family dinners he would say, "Boy tell your Aunt Panthea what you're going to be when you grow up?" Then I would say, "I'm going to be a doctor." Then he would say, "Okay, now go play boy." His request and my response would be repeated as often as he felt like initiating it.

At the time, it seemed to me to be a daily ritual. As the vision of being a physician was established in my head, I began to respond by determining and following college preparatory courses in high school. I majored in biology (a pre-medical focus) in college and eventually entered and completed medical school.

What are the Leading Causes of LIFE?

An interesting thing about this story is, in my junior year of high school, I was advised by my counselor that " I did not have what it took to be a physician." He said in other words, I was not smart enough to handle the sciences necessary to succeed in medicine. When I told my father what the counselor said, he said to me, "Boy what did I tell you you're going to be when you grow up?" My response was the same it had always been, "You said, I'm going to be a doctor." Then he said, "that's right, now go play boy."

I remember applying to several colleges. Because we didn't have a lot of money my first choice was our state university. I did get accepted. However, the acceptance letter said something like this, "Congratulations! You have been accepted into _____ State University. However, based on your academic record to date and the recommendation of your counselor, we recommend you not major in 'pre-med' but in _____ _____." The letter actually named a major that the school felt was less academically rigorous. It was the same suggestion my counselor had made when he told me I couldn't handle the sciences of pre-med.

Needless to say, I did not go to the State University. I went to one of the schools that accepted me unconditionally, Howard University. I chose a pre-med major, biology. I achieved my Bachelor of Science degree, spent a year in graduate school, was accepted attended and completed medical school.

After I graduated from medical school, I went back to my high school to visit the counselor who told me I did not have what it took to be a physician. My message to him was, don't ever let your preconceived notions of who it takes and what it takes to accomplish something serve to discourage or dissuade young people (who don't fit your notions) away from their dreams.

This personal account embodies all four of the life generating principles outlined in this book. From childhood my father and mother made me know and believe that **I was made by God, and everything God made, works**. They made it clear to me that despite what that counselor said, I had what it took to be a physician.

My father was a 'believer.' He knew about the limitlessness of spiritual strength, resolve, belief and faith. He was inherently aware of the principle, **"Everything God made has everything it needs to work."** So he kept telling me, "You can do it." I remember vividly, he never ever wavered on this point.

Further, my parents were workers. They believed in working and the results of work. At one point my father had three jobs. He worked at a tool company, a clothing store and a funeral home. He learned valuable lessons from each that benefited him, his family and others. His behavior was consistent with the third principle of this book, **"Everything God made was made to do work."**

There is one thing with which all of the siblings agree, that is, our father placed a priority on his family. We had a wonderful relationship with him. Not only did he have a great relationship with his family, he had many good relationships outside of us. He was actively involved in church, community and political affairs. He knew the value of relationships. He developed good relationships that not only benefited him while alive, but have continued to benefit his family long after he made his transition back to the spirit realm. Once again his life reflected one of the principles governing the life functioning of the universe. In this case, it was the fourth, **"Everything God made was made to work at its highest and best in relationship with everything else God made."**

My father seemed to live by these principles without identifying them as such. By most criteria and observers, he was considered a 'successful' person. He was certainly considered successful by all who knew him. By way of example, he passed on to his children a desire to live the same way.

My hope is, now that you have read this book, you are inspired even motivated, to live at your highest and best. At a minimum, I hope you are a little more informed or, you've had your perspective broadened.

Certainly it won't hurt, and, I believe it will definitely help you to maximize each moment when you adopt these principles and allow them to govern how you live your life.

Life is a wonderful thing given to us by a wonderful Creator. God is life. Everything that God made reflects that life. This means, it works, it has all it needs to work, it has a work assignment from which it does not vary and, it works at its highest and best through relationship.

A Prescription of Living at Your Highest and Best

You and I are made by God.
- ✓ **We were made to work.**
- ✓ **We have everything we need to work.**
- ✓ **We were made to do work.**
- ✓ **We were made to work at our highest and best through relationship with each other and everything else God made.**

I'm hopeful that the words of this book will find their way into the hearts and minds of as many young people as possible. My vision is, they will be sufficiently impacted to change the way they think about themselves and others and as a result, I will have played a part in enhancing the movement away from the death orientation that seems to characterize this world, and towards the life orientation that would bring more joy for all of us.

May God bless and prosper you with abundant life.

www.ingramcontent.com/pod-product-compliance
Lightning Source LLC
Chambersburg PA
CBHW061944070426
42450CB00007BA/1047

www.ingramcontent.com/pod-product-compliance
Lightning Source LLC
Chambersburg PA
CBHW061944070426
42450CB00007BA/1047